STRATEGIES
FOR
STRUGGLING READERS

Written by

Jo Fitzpatrick

Editors: Kelly Gunzenhauser and Jennifer Taylor
Illustrator: Jenny Campbell
Designer/ Production: Barbara Peterson
Art Director: Moonhee Pak
Project Director: Betsy Morris, PhD

Table of Contents

Introduction

Meeting the needs of struggling readers is an ongoing challenge that schools and teachers have grown accustomed to facing. Within the past few years, scientific research has dictated much of the basis for new approaches to reading instruction. With the U.S. government mandating the use of this research-based approach, school districts have been actively adopting sounder and more balanced reading programs. Staff development also now heavily emphasizes teaching practices that implement the five components of reading instruction outlined by the National Reading Council (phonemic awareness, phonics, vocabulary, fluency, and comprehension).

Though schools offer programs designed to give additional support to struggling readers, about one student in three still has trouble reading. Many remedial programs may be subjecting students to the same strategies and techniques that were not effective in their regular classrooms. Many struggling readers continue to experience the "been there, done that" syndrome and continue to falter, resulting in negative attitudes and behavior problems that further hinder their learning.

Strategies for Struggling Readers takes a unique approach that exposes students to brain-based learning. This resource offers students the opportunity to learn how the brain works and participate in brain-based instructional activities. By seeing how brain research ties into everyday learning, students develop a better understanding of how learning occurs and recognize their role in the learning process. Instruction in brain-based learning theory helps struggling readers discover the following information:

* How people learn

* How the brain processes information

* What must happen for learning to become permanent

* How chunking information increases working memory capacity

* What types of practice are necessary for retention

* Why time is a significant factor

* Their role in learning

* The importance of commitment

Introduction

The underlying philosophy of this approach is to deal openly and honestly with students' reading problems and to discuss how to address them. The activities have been specifically designed to improve struggling students' reading and overall academic skills. With this approach, students are always told why they are doing an activity and how it will help them. When students, especially those who have been exposed to the same unsuccessful instructional techniques, see this connection, they are very cooperative and willing to put forth their best efforts. Instruction becomes a mutual effort for students and the teacher as students begin to feel like they are part of the instructional process and realize that their attitudes and commitment are part of the solution.

The teacher is a crucial factor in the learning process, so teachers need to have strong backgrounds, understand the rationale behind their instruction, and know how it will improve student learning. With that in mind, Strategies for Struggling Readers also provides teachers with a knowledge base about teaching reading. Because it provides this support, this book is the ideal resource for teachers seeking to help their students who are still struggling to learn how to read.

Research-Based Principles for Struggling Readers

There are four research-based design principles that must be part of any successful intervention program (Allington, 2006). The suggested intervention program in this resource incorporates these four basic principles:

Principle #1 — Provide expanded opportunities for students to read, and help them become engaged in that reading.

Research indicates that engaged students spend 500% more time reading than disengaged students (Guthrie, 2004). Reading volume has been widely neglected in intervention programs. Therefore, it is imperative to increase allotted reading time for struggling readers, and to find ways to make sure that students are engaged in their reading during that time.

Principle #2 — Match text to struggling readers' actual reading levels.

Research has proven that using texts matched to struggling readers' actual reading levels results in greater gains, especially for students at the lowest levels of proficiency (Guthrie, Schafer, and Huang, 2001). Ideally, struggling readers should spend 80% of their school days working with texts that they can read with 90% accuracy. However, it is very common to see grade-appropriate texts assigned to struggling readers. If these readers are to succeed, intervention needs to be based on materials that they can read accurately, fluently, and with good comprehension.

Principle #3 — Provide systematic and explicit strategy instruction.

Struggling readers need systematic and explicit instruction (in all areas of reading) provided by expert teachers who understand the beginning reading process. While one-on-one tutoring is the most powerful intervention, small-group instruction for students with similar needs has also proven beneficial.

Principle #4 — Ensure articulation between intervention providers and classroom teachers.

Research indicates that there must be communication between intervention providers and classroom teachers, and that students must experience a balanced and coherent instructional program with an array of lessons and activities.

Recommended Instructional Model for Reading Intervention

Reading intervention programs can follow many different schedules and include many different components, or segments. Below is a list of recommended segments to include when assisting struggling readers. Suggested time allotments should be adjusted according to these factors:

✺ Whether your school or district has an existing intervention program to follow
✺ Whether you may pull students out of the classroom for intervention
✺ Whether you can group students according to reading difficulties
✺ Students' ages and abilities
✺ The time you or the intervention teacher/staff have available

Segment #1   Self-Selected Reading and Structured Writing
Reading and writing at students' independent reading levels — 20 minutes

Self-Selected Reading

Self-selected, active reading sets a supportive tone for the instructional session. Having students choose familiar stories or books that are at their independent reading levels increases the amount of reading that students can accomplish. Pay special attention to reading rates during this segment. If a student **reads very slowly**, the text may be too difficult. Provide easier text and ask the student to read a second time for fluency. If a student **reads word-by-word**, use chunking strategies (see page 25 of the *My Brain Teaching Script*) and emphasize seeing more than one word at a time. Read the passage with the student, group appropriate words together, and then allow the student to read it alone. If a student **reads too fast**, causing inaccuracies or decreased comprehension, invite the student to read the text like a turtle or a snail (slowly).

During this segment, students should use the Give Me Five—*S* cycle as they read. Students should **select** their own reading materials, **scan** the pictures to preview the story, **skim** the story to find and write down a word of interest from each page, **summarize** what the story was about, and reread the story for **speed** (fluency). Use **Structured Writing** (page 7) to monitor comprehension. Finally, the teacher's job during this segment is to facilitate: to question, observe, model, monitor reading, and encourage students to verbalize strategies they use.

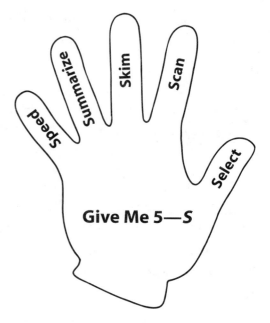

Give Me 5—S

Structured Writing

Following Self-Selected Reading, students should write about or otherwise reflect upon what they have read. Have them complete copies of the **Reader's Review reproducible (page 12)** by responding to the prompts, scoring the book, and writing the reason for the score. (File these so that students can use others' reviews to help them choose books.) Each student can also write a brief reader's theater piece of a scene, draw pictures to complete a visual story sequence, audio- or videotape himself or herself reading out scenes, or change one story element (such as the ending, the setting, or a character). Other ideas include letting students choose a story and chorally read it as a class, or collaboratively write a rap, a song, or even stage directions for an interpretive dance.

Segment #2   Strategy and Skill Development
Explicit instruction in phonics, grammar, and word-attack strategies—30 minutes

Assuming someone has assessed students' reading capabilities, use the assessments to address each student's problem reading areas. Students may be aware of their difficulties, but they don't often know what to do about them. Review each student's assessment results individually to make him or her aware of strengths and areas needing attention, and then implement directed strategy and skill development instruction with emphasis on brain-based learning. Refer to the **objective bullets** in the activities section (pages 44-126) for specific ways to address different weaknesses.

Segment #3   Guided Reading
Direct teaching of reading strategies and content standards—30 minutes

During this segment, make content more comprehensible through direct instruction of strategies that will ensure active reading. These strategies are outlined on page 8 and are represented by pictures on the **Strategies Bookmark Reproducibles** (page 13). They combine elements of phonemic awareness, phonics, vocabulary, fluency, and comprehension instruction and demonstrate applying word-attack skills and using context to gain meaning. Help students internalize the strategies by introducing the bookmark, choosing skill-based activities to teach its strategies, and relating them to student reading selections.

Strategies Bookmark Instruction for Unknown Words

When students come across unfamiliar words, do not tell them the words. Direct them to the Strategies Bookmark. Describe how each picture prompt relates to a strategy, and provide sufficient guidance about using the strategies. After students are familiar with the picture prompts, encourage them to refer to their bookmarks as they read independently. Note that many strategies have some overlap, as do the activities listed for teaching each one.

Strategy	Picture Prompt	Ask students to try the following steps:	Activities
*1 **Does it make sense?**		• Think about what you already know about the subject. • Guess what the word might be. • Consider if that word makes sense in the sentence.	• Click and Clank; Give It Meaning; See It, Say It; Letter Snatcher
*2 **Look for key words and clues.**		• Look for key words in the sentence (nouns and descriptive words). • Look for clues in the pictures in the book.	• Word Association; What's Missing?; The Missing Link; Relationship Box; See It, Say It; Collaborative Reading
*3 **Listen to how it sounds.**		• Identify the beginning, middle, and ending sounds of the word. • Sound out the letters. • Guess the word and say it in the sentence. • Consider if it sounds right.	• All phonemic awareness activities, Short Vowel Response Cards, Short Vowel Sound Puzzle, Syllable Spot, Vowel Combination Response Cards
*4 **Look for little words in big words.**		• Look for hidden words to help pronounce the bigger, unfamiliar word.	• Scavenger Hunt, Which Word Doesn't Belong?
*5 **Search for similarities.**		• Look and listen for similarities among words. • Consider if words sound the same. • See if words have the same letter patterns.	• Any activity that trains students to look for spelling patterns in words is relevant: Rhyming Riddles, Rhyming Words, Speedball Vowels, Word Line, Short Vowel Flashcards, Word Swap, What Makes Long Vowels Long?, Silent Race, Switcheroo, Word Sorts, Long Vowel Classification, Find and List
*6 **Try a popper.**		• Sound out the first letter of an unfamiliar word. • Continue reading the rest of the sentence. • See if the word "pops" into your head!	• Poppers, Letter Snatcher, see also page 29 of the My Brain Teaching Script
*7 **Backtrack and read again.**		• Reread the sentence. • Notice clues you missed the first time.	• Collaborative Reading; Criss-Cross Sentences; What's Missing?; Give It Meaning; The Missing Link; Letter Snatcher
*8 **Skip it and go on.**		• Skip the unfamiliar word. • Keep reading the sentence. • Use the sentence context to understand the word.	• What's Missing?, Give It Meaning, The Missing Link, Letter Snatcher

Segment #4 Common Problem Areas
Supervised assessment and correction of skills—20 minutes

Use this segment (and the Self-Selected Reading segment) for one-on-one diagnosis and instruction. This is the most valuable segment of the intervention program because you will address specific needs. During these assessment segments, observe and diagnose individual problems and demonstrate corrective strategies. The common problem areas segment helps students as they work individually or in small groups on areas in which they need additional practice. Common problems can include things like trouble with unknown words, ignoring punctuation, or irregular reading rates. Depending on their needs, students may be working on phonics, language development, silent reading comprehension, or reading fluency. This is the perfect time to incorporate additional support programs that are available at your school.

Segment #5 Self-Assessment
Goal setting and evaluation — 5–10 minutes

Obviously, reading and understanding text is difficult for struggling readers. To reach these students, you must replace their failures with successes. Self-assessments help students see their progress and understand that their attitudes and hard work result in positive change. The self-assessment reproducibles (pages 14–15) emphasize work habits, skills and strategies, attitudes, and individual goal setting.

Work with each student to choose a goal for the week, such as *I will look for silent e in words* or *I will increase my reading speed.* Be sure each selected goal relates to the skill and activities being emphasized, and to each student. During this segment, refer to students' goals and acknowledge their efforts to meet those goals. At the end of the instructional period, have students assess how they did that day using the self-assessment reproducibles. Make sure students have time to concentrate on a particular area and complete the self-assessment forms before moving to new goals. Students need to internalize the assessment criteria before they choose their own goals.

You may choose to share assessments with classroom teachers (if they are not the ones providing intervention) to demonstrate students' achievements and changing attitudes. Students may want to revisit their assessments to see how far they have come. For these reasons, it is a good idea to take a few minutes at the beginning of the intervention program to have students make self-assessment folders in which to keep the forms.

Segment #6 Journal Writing

A dialogue about the learning process — 10–15 minutes

Incorporating journal writing helps students develop and build on written language skills and gives students a chance to apply these skills and incorporate self-assessment. Depending on students' needs, entries can serve different purposes.

Initially, you will write the entries, focusing on how each day's activity helps students improve their reading. As students recognize how their participation affects their progress, they can write their own entries. Prior to the instructional block, write a starter prompt on the board, such as *Today I _____. It helped me _____.* Cover the prompt until the end of the session, then have students copy and respond to it. Eventually, use journal writing to dialogue with students about their hard work, attitudes, and progress, and to give them opportunities to write self-assessment entries in addition to using the self-assessment reproducibles. Consider asking students' permission to share their journal entries with classroom teachers to help relate their progress.

Partner Journaling

In order to be successful, students need to feel safe in their environment and connected to their peers and teachers. When struggling readers connect with their teachers and classmates, they tend to take more responsibility for the environment in that classroom. Partner journaling can be used to foster these connections because it gives students opportunities to share about themselves in a deeper way. Before introducing partner journaling, make topic cards. Each week, write six or seven topics on an index card for each student. Let students keep the cards in their journals for reference. These topics should be relevant, interesting, and of a reflective nature. (See **Journal Writing Topics**, page 11, for examples.) Then conduct journaling sessions in this order:

1. To introduce journaling, model writing an entry. Choose a topic and write it on a transparency. Then write some superficial things about it.

2. Next, model how to "go deep inside yourself" by reflecting on why you feel as you do, why the topic is important to you, and how it has affected you and others.

3. Then, ask students to choose topics from their topic cards or make up their own topics.

4. Ask some volunteers to share their topics. Model how to ask pertinent questions that expand each idea or make it more personal. Let other students ask questions.

5. Once students have adequate experience with this process, have them choose partners (different partners each time). Partners should not have the same topics.

6. Encourage students to ask each other *who, what, where, when,* and *why* questions to help them expand their topics. Partners should "dig down deep" to share how they think and feel.

7. Students should then write their entries independently.

Journal entries do not need to be lengthy. The goal is to give students a means to connect socially and emotionally; style, spelling, and structure should be taught in directed writing lessons. (Punctuation may be addressed because it can interfere with readability.)

Journal Writing Topics

What makes you happy? Share one of your happiest experiences.	How do you feel about yourself at this moment in time?	What talent were you given for which you are grateful?	If you could have anything in the world, what would it be?
Describe an activity that makes you feel good about yourself.	What makes you sad? Share one of your saddest experiences.	Describe a time when you were able to help someone.	What goals do you have for your future?
Share ways in which you have changed over the last few years.	What makes you feel lonely? Share a time when you felt lonely.	Share a time when you were very proud of yourself.	Write about something you strongly believe in.
If you could change something about yourself, what would it be?	What do your friends like about you?	Describe something you want to do and tell why you want to do it.	Tell about the progress you are making in class. What are you learning?
Share your interests and hobbies. What do you like to do?	Write about your best quality.	Share what you want to be. Why do you want to be that?	What do you think makes a good friend?

Name: _____   Date: _____

Reader's Review

Book Title: _____

Author: _____

What was the book about?

WHAT? _____

_____

_____

So... _____

_____

_____

THEN _____

_____

_____

How would you rate this book? (Circle one.)

Reason for score: _____

_____

_____

_____

Strategies For Struggling Readers © 2007 Creative Teaching Press

Strategies Bookmark Reproducibles

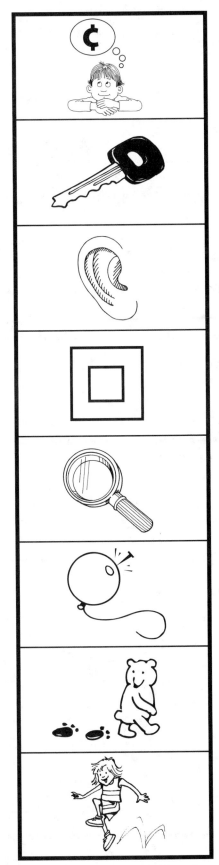 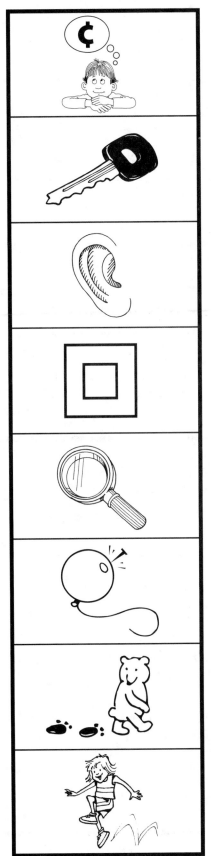

Work Habits Self-Assessment

Goal:_____

Monday _____ Tuesday _____ Wednesday _____

Thursday _____ Friday _____

SW = Super Worker!
ST = Super Thinker!
SPS = Super Problem Solver!

Scored by _____ Date _____

How I Think I Did

Goal:_____

Monday _____ Tuesday _____ Wednesday _____

Thursday _____ Friday _____

1 = I learned from my mistake.
2 = I used a "popper."
3 = I solved a problem.
4 = I used a strategy.
5 = I thought about what made sense.

Scored by _____ Date _____

Strategies For Struggling Readers © 2007 Creative Teaching Press

Attitude

Goal:_____

1. I was eager to do my best. **2.** I was energetic. **3.** I showed what I know.

4. I was enthusiastic about my work. **5.** I was attentive and answered questions.

6. I need to work on _____

Monday _____ Tuesday _____ Wednesday _____

Thursday _____ Friday _____

Assessed by _____ Date _____

How I Think I Did

Goal:_____

+ I worked hard at my goal. √ I could have done more. – I did not think enough about my goal.

Monday _____ Tuesday _____ Wednesday _____ Thursday _____ Friday _____

List of goals:

I will work on fluency.
I will use my reading strategies.
I will catch my mistakes.
I will look for clues in words.
I will use context to get meaning.
I will practice my reading.
I will show a good attitude.

I will finish all of my work.
I will stay on task.
I will listen and follow directions.
I will focus on what I am doing.
I will keep on trying and not give up.
I will think about what I do well.
I will congratulate myself!

Assessed by _____ Date _____

Teaching Students about Brain-Based Learning

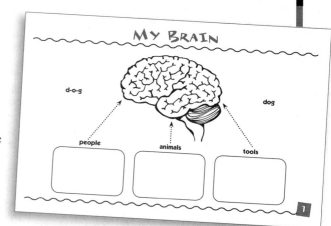

Brain-based learning techniques can positively influence students' understanding of the learning process and increase their motivation and personal commitment. This simple approach to learning and memory can be the tool that will make a difference. Giving students knowledge about how to use brain-based learning techniques to improve their reading can lead to better overall academic performance. The *My Brain Booklet* **(pages 34–43)**, used in conjunction with the *My Brain Teaching Script* **(pages 18–33)**, is an interactive tool to which students add words and graphics to personalize the information.

Implementing My Brain Booklet and Teaching Script

Materials

✳ The interactive *My Brain Booklet* **(pages 34–43)** teaches students about memory and learning. Each student needs his or her own copy to personalize.

✳ The *My Brain Teaching Script* **(pages 18–33)** is a word-for-word model of the instruction. Read and discuss this with students to introduce and explain the graphics on each page of the *My Brain Booklet*.

✳ Create **transparencies of the booklet** and use **an overhead projector** and **erasable markers** so that you can model how to draw and color the booklet. Invite students to complete their pages as you do the same on the transparency.

✳ Students need access to **crayons, colored pencils, or markers** (red, green, black, blue, and yellow).

Procedure and Schedule

As you start training, provide an orientation session. Then divide up the different parts of the booklet according to what your schedule will accommodate. You can break the training into sessions as listed below, or you can complete all of the training in one day and review for several days afterward. Read aloud the blue text in the script, and encourage student participation. Teacher directions are in *black*.

Below is a sample training schedule. If you teach the *My Brain Booklet* over several days, use the schedule to help you decide how many days you need. But you do **not** have to spread out training. If you decide to teach the entire *My Brain Booklet* in one day, the suggested session groupings show logical places where students can take breaks. If you have one day of training, remember that students need to practice the material 18–24 hours after learning it in order to retain the information. To review, let students complete any activities a second time.

Session #1–My Brain, Front-Brain and Back-Brain Learning
* Orientation Session (Explain that students are there to work on reading and learning better.)
* *My Brain Booklet*, pages 1–4
* Duration: 20 minutes

Session #2–How the Brain Works, Sensory Input
* *My Brain Booklet*, pages 5–8
* Duration: 20 minutes

Session #3–Short-Term Memory, Working Memory
* *My Brain Booklet*, pages 9–12
* Duration: 25 minutes

Session #4–Long-Term Memory, This is How I Remember
* *My Brain Booklet*, pages 13–16
* Duration: 20 minutes

Session #5–What Can I Do, What I Will Do?, What Teachers and Students Can Do
* *My Brain Booklet*, pages 17–20
* Duration: 25 minutes

Session #6–Self-Selected Reading and Structured Writing
* Have students do **Self-Selected Reading (page 6).**
* Model **Structured Writing (page 7)**, or conduct a structured writing time if students are aware of the procedure.
* Duration: 40 minutes

Session #7–Self Assessment
* Make **self-assessment folders (page 9)**.
* Have students complete one self-assessment reproducible.
* Duration: 20 minutes

At this point, integrate the other segments from the **Recommended Instructional Model (page 6)** and the **Reading Activities (pages 44–126)** as needed.

Session #1: My Brain

My Brain Booklet, page 1
(See reproducible page 34)

If you could open up your head and take a picture, this is what you would see. This is what the brain looks like. Why do we each have a brain? What does the brain do? Your brain is what makes everything in your body work, and it helps you think and learn. We are going to talk about how your brain works. I will ask you to do some funny things, like coloring, drawing, and even singing! These things will help you understand your brain. *(Especially older students may balk at some of the exercises, such as coloring and singing, because they may seem more appropriate for younger grades. If so, acknowledge that students may feel silly at first, but then explain that the silliness they feel will actually do a lot to help them to remember and make sense of the information they are learning. Finally, remember that if you have fun, students will have fun with you.)*

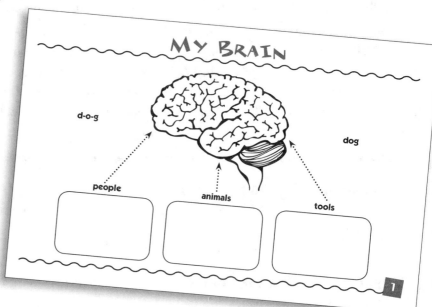

Look at the picture of the brain again. The brain is made up of many different parts, or lobes, and each part has a special job to do, from helping you breathe and move to recognizing danger. For example, you use different parts of the brain to name different objects. Find the word *people* on your page, and draw some people under the word. If I asked you the name of your teacher, what part of the brain would you use? Use a crayon to trace the arrow that points to that part of the brain.

Now, find the word *animals*, draw a picture of any animal, and trace the arrow. Point to the part of the brain that you would use if I asked you to name an animal that has spots and a long neck. *(Call on a student to name the animal.)*

Under the word *tools*, draw a picture of a tool, and trace that arrow. Show me the part of the brain that you would use if I asked you to name the tool you drew. *(Call on a student to point to that part of the brain and then name the tool he or she illustrated.)*

To say the names of people, animals, and tools, you use three different parts of your brain. When you learn to read, you also use different parts of your brain to hear and write sounds, to put sounds together to make words, and to remember whole words. When you learn to read, you use the front part of your brain and read words one letter at a time. To learn to read the word *d-o-g*, your brain actually looks at each letter and sound, /d/ /o/ /g/, to read the word. But in order to read faster—to look at a whole word and immediately know that it is the word *dog*—you have to use the back of your brain. Let's do an activity, and then we will look at the next page to learn more about front-brain reading and back-brain reading.

My Brain Booklet, page 2
(See reproducible page 34)
Turn to page 2 of your booklet and look at the question: *What does the brain look like to you?* Draw a picture of what the brain looks like. Why do you think you are drawing this picture?

Session *1 (cont.): Front and Back Brain

My Brain Booklet, page 3
(See reproducible page 35)

Let's look at the difference between front-brain reading and back-brain reading. In order to read these hyphenated sentences, the front part of the brain looks at every letter. *(Read the first message slowly, almost sounding it out.)* Let me show you how reading every letter can slow you down. On the first line in your booklet, write your name, but put a hyphen between each letter. *(On a transparency, write your name with hyphens.)* Did you have to think about the letters and remember to put in the hyphens?

Now, look at the bottom of the page. The same message is written without hyphens. When reading takes place in the back of the brain, it sounds like this. *(Read the message fluently.)* Write your name on the line like you usually do, without hyphens. See how much faster that is? Why is it faster to write this way? *(Pause for answers.)* Yes, when you don't have to stop and think about the letters and the hyphens, the writing is faster. You just wrote your name automatically—without even thinking. Well, that's how reading happens when the back of the brain is used. So, your job is to move your reading from the front of your brain to the back. You're going to train your brain to do this by learning and practicing some reading strategies.

My Brain Booklet, page 4
(See reproducible page 35)

Look at the two people. How are they different? *(Pause for answers.)* Right, one is younger. Circle the person whom you think reads faster. Who did you circle? *(Call on a student to answer. Most students will say that the older person reads faster.)* When might the younger person read faster? *(Answers may be When the older person is just learning English or When the younger person is a genius.)*

(Pair students with partners.) Cover everything except sentence 1a. One of you should read that sentence aloud while the other listens. *(Pause.)* Now, read sentence 1b, without hyphens. *(Pause.)* Which sentence was easier to read? *(Pause.)* Let the other partner read sentences 2a and 2b in the same way and decide which was easier. *(Pause.)* Why were the sentences without hyphens easier?

Session #2: How the Brain Works

My Brain Booklet, page 5
(See reproducible page 36)

It's important to understand how the brain works, because that helps you train your brain to learn better. Page 5 shows a picture of how information passes through the brain until it becomes part of your memory. Use your green crayon to trace the arrows that point to the right. They show the paths that information follows when it moves. Notice that at every point, information can fall out of your brain. Use your red crayon to trace all of the arrows that point down, except for the curved arrow. The

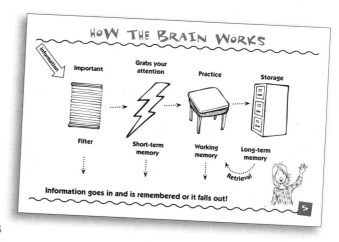

arrows that point down show the paths that information takes when it falls out. If information falls out, it is not learned. *(The graphic is shown at this point to give students the big picture. Each segment of the brain will be discussed in the following pages of the booklet.)*

My Brain Booklet, page 6
(See reproducible page 36)

Practice finding information for your brain by closing your eyes and taking an imaginary walk across the playground to see what your senses pick up. Think about what you see, hear, smell, and touch on the playground. Can you think of anything you might taste? Draw a picture of something each of your senses will notice. *(Pause while students imagine and draw.)* Now that your senses have taken in this information, your brain decides

whether this information drops out or moves ahead. On the next page, we will find out how that happens.

Session #2 (cont): Sensory Input

My Brain Booklet, page 7
(See reproducible page 37)

Let's take a look at how your brain remembers things. You take in information from your environment, which is everything around you. Look at the picture and tell me how you take in information. *(Pause for answers.)* That's right, eyes and ears show that you see things and hear things. What other ways do we take in information? *(Pause for answers.)* Yes, you use all of your senses: touch, taste, and smell. Now, imagine what a person with extra-powerful senses would look like, and draw a picture of that person.

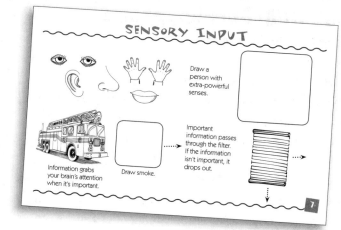

Your brain takes in 40,000 bits of information a second, but you certainly don't remember all of that. Imagine that you hear a siren. Color the fire engine red to show where you imagine the siren comes from. Hearing a siren is not unusual. Most of the time, you probably don't pay much attention. There is no reason to remember every siren that you hear. But what if you hear a siren and smell smoke? Draw smoke near the fire engine. If you smell smoke, you may be concerned that the fire is near, so the siren becomes more important. Because the siren is now important, it passes through the brain's filter. The filter is like window blinds. Color the window blinds yellow. When information is important, the filter opens so that information can pass into your memory like light through the blinds. Use your green crayon to trace the arrow on the far right of the page to show that the information passed through the filter. If information is not important, the filter closes and the information drops out. Use your red crayon to trace the arrow that shows where information can drop out.

My Brain Booklet, page 8
(See reproducible page 37)

Now, demonstrate how your filter works. Make a fist with your hand. This is your filter. As you look at each picture, if the picture is of something that interests you, open your fist. If a picture does not interest you, close your fist. Since everybody's interests are different, some fists may be open while others are closed. Now, circle the items that made you open your fist. *(Say the name of each picture: candy, shark, line, trash, onion, square, race car, kitten.)* What made your filter open? Why? What made your filter close? Why? When you are finished, draw and color a picture of something that would make you open your fist.

Session #3: Short-Term Memory

My Brain Booklet, page 9
(See reproducible page 38)

Did you know that you have three kinds of memory? Information has to get past the filter and then go through these three kinds of memory if it is going to be learned. On page 9, we see what happens after information passes through the filter (the one that acts like window blinds). It moves to the first kind of memory, which is your short-term memory. This is called short-term memory because it holds information for a very short time—about

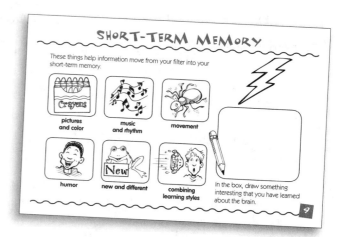

18 seconds. Short-term memory acts like a lightening flash. Something has to happen to get the brain's attention so that the information does not drop out. What do you think gets the brain to pay attention?

* **Pictures** and **colors** get the brain's attention. That is why you are drawing, coloring, and tracing things. If information is written with different colors or is shown with pictures, the brain is more likely to notice. Color the box of crayons to remind you that the brain likes color and pictures.

* **Music** (*Sing this word.*) and **rhythm** (*Clap your hands.*) get the brain's attention. If you want to learn spelling words, try singing the letters. (*Sing the letters in the word* **brains** *to the tune of "Happy Birthday." Ask students to join in.*) Use a crayon to trace the musical notes to show that music grabs your brain's attention.

* **Movement** gets the brain's attention. Using your body makes an impression and improves learning. For example, how many of you remember the words and motions to "The Itsy Bitsy Spider?" (*Sing the following song and do the hand motions. Invite students to join in.*)

  The itsy, bitsy spider went up the waterspout. (*Touch your right index finger to your left thumb and then your left index finger to your right thumb, making a crawling motion.*)

  Down came the rain and washed the spider out. (*Raise your hands and wiggle your fingers as you lower them to simulate rain.*)

  Out came the sun and dried up all the rain. (*Raise your arms and touch your hands together to make a big circle.*)

  And the itsy, bitsy spider went up the spout again. (*Repeat the index finger and thumb "crawling" motion.*)

Color the wiggly spider.

✳ **Humor** gets the brain's attention. Just like you remember a good joke, the brain remembers information when it is presented in a funny way.

What does a brain do when it sees a friend? Gives a brain wave!

✳ **Something new or different** gets the brain's attention. The brain tends to remember new, unusual information. If I told you that frogs eat their old skin after they shed it, you probably wouldn't forget something like that!

✳ **Using more than one learning style** gets the brain's attention. There are three **learning styles:** visual, auditory, and kinesthetic, or seeing, hearing, and moving. If you learn something in more than one way, you will remember it better. For example, if I say *Pie in the face!* you hear it. But, if I say *Pie in the face!* and throw a pie at someone, you hear it and see it. And if I say *Pie in the face!* and hit you with a pie, you will hear it, see it, and try to move away from it.

✳ Next to the pencil, draw a picture showing something interesting that you have learned about the brain. Look back over your booklet for ideas.

My Brain Booklet, page 10
(See reproducible page 38)

Look at the writing and the pictures.
• Circle the television you prefer.
• Circle the math lesson you prefer.
• Circle the reading lesson you prefer.
• Circle the transportation you prefer.
• Circle the shoe you prefer.
• Circle the cat you prefer.

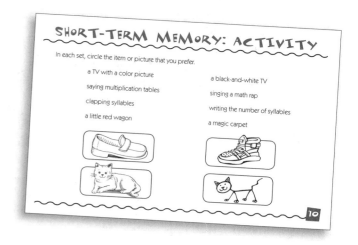

(Discuss which items and pictures students selected, and why. Paraphrase students' answers, using the terms color, music, movement, humor, and new to explain why these things got their brains' attention.)

Session #3 (cont): Working Memory

My Brain Booklet, page 11
(See reproducible page 39)

(Teach this segment in the same session as short-term memory or as its own session.)

You have looked at how information grabs your brain's attention and goes through the filter into your short-term memory. What would happen if information did not grab the brain's attention? *(Pause for answer.)* Yes, the information would fall out. What can you do to make sure the information doesn't fall out? *(Pause for answers.)* If the information is interesting and you give your brain some help, the information moves to the second kind of memory—the working memory.

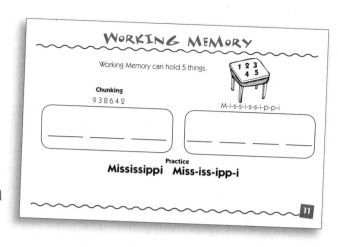

The working memory is represented by a picture of a desk because you have to use this kind of memory to work with information (like you use a desk for schoolwork) if you are going to remember it. The desk only holds a limited amount of information. At your age, the working memory can remember about five things at a time. If too much is in your working memory, new information falls out and is not learned. But there are some tricks to help your working memory learn and remember more things.

Chunking

Listen to these numbers and try to remember them: 9, 3, 8, 6, 4, 2. Write those six numbers on the line on the picture of the desk. Remember that you can store five things in your working memory, but I gave you six numbers. How can you shrink what you have to remember? *(Pause for answer.)* Try combining the six numbers (9, 3, 8, 6, 4, 2) to make three numbers (93, 86, and 42). Write these three numbers on the three lines. This is called *chunking.* You can chunk information together to make it smaller.

Let's try chunking with something else. Spell *Mississippi*—M-i-s-s-i-s-s-i-p-p-i. How many letters is that? *(Pause for answer.)* How can you possibly remember 11 letters if your working memory can only hold about five things at a time? That's right, you can chunk it. What if you spell Mississippi like this, Miss – iss – ipp - i? *(Write it this way on a transparency.)* How many chunks or groups do you have to remember? *(Pause for answer.)*

Right, there are only four chunks. Do you see a spelling pattern? There's an *i* followed by two double *letters*. Do you see anything else? Are any of the chunks alike? *(Pause for answer.)* Right, the letters *iss* are repeated two times in the word. We've chunked the information. Under the hyphenated word M-i-s-s-i-s-s-i-p-p-i, write the word *Mississippi* in chunks.

Practice

Besides chunking, there are other things you can do to help things remain in your working memory. To make sure that the chunked spelling of *Mississippi* stays in your memory, you have to practice it. Practice doesn't have to be boring. Let's be silly and spell the word using different voices. Use a giant voice to spell it. *(Spell the word with a loud voice, using the "chunked" spelling pattern.)* Now, spell it with a teeny, tiny mouse voice. *(Spell the word with a soft, squeaky voice.)* Use a really high voice. *(Spell the word with a high voice.)* Now, use a deep, low voice. *(Spell the word with a deep voice.)* Use your regular voice to spell Mississippi. *(Spell the word.)* Use your finger to write it on top of your desk. *(Demonstrate.)* Spell it and tap your feet in rhythm. *(Demonstrate.)* Spell *Mississippi* and stand up every time you say the letter *i*. *(Do this with students, and let them suggest some other silly things to do.)* This feels silly, but since it is different from what we usually do, that helps the brain remember it.

Do you think that you will remember how to spell *Mississippi*? Why? If you don't practice, what happens? *(Pause for answer.)* Use your red crayon to draw a line through the word *Mississippi* to show that if you don't practice, the information will fall out and you will forget how to spell *Mississippi*. If you do practice, what will happen? Use your green crayon to draw a green arrow from the chunked word to the right-hand edge of the page.

My Brain Booklet, page 12
(See reproducible page 39)

Look at page 12 of the booklet. You should see two groups of numbers, the word *Massachusetts*, and a group of five words. Think about how you would chunk each of these to make sure they remained in your working memory. In your booklet, write a solution for remembering each of these. *(Let students share answers, then explain the solutions.)* For the numbers 1, 8, 5, 6, 7, 0 you could chunk them into three numbers: 18, 56, and 70. You could chunk 2, 1, 4, 3, 8, 6, 9 into a telephone number: 214-3869. To spell *Massachusetts*, you could chunk the letters: *Mass–a–chu–setts*. To remember *school, story, elephant, banana,* and *trampoline*, you could chunk the words into a sentence, like *Today at school, I read a story about an elephant eating a banana on a trampoline*. What kinds of practice could you use to help you remember even better? *(Students may suggest singing or clapping. Suggest other ways to practice: drawing a picture of the sentence, pretending to dial the phone numbers, or learning about Massachusetts.)*

Session #4: Long-Term Memory

My Brain Booklet, page 13
(See reproducible page 40)

Look back at page 5 in your booklet. You can
see that next to the working memory desk is a file
cabinet that represents long-term memory. On
pages 11–12, you can see how to help your
working memory work with information and move
it closer to your long-term memory, where you
store everything you have learned. Spelling
Mississippi is a good example because you
probably remember how to spell it. (*Let a
volunteer spell Mississippi.*)

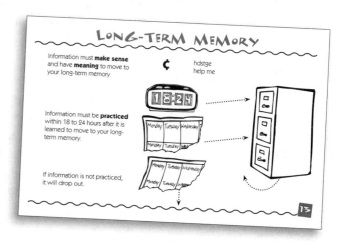

Sense and Meaning

 In order for the information to move on to your long-term memory, it has to make sense. Use any color
to trace the cents sign. Look at the nonsense word. Do you think it will be easier to remember that
nonsense word or the two words under the nonsense word? Cross out the word or words you think will
be harder to remember. Which word or words didn't you cross out? Why? (*Pause for answer.*) Those
letters spell two words that we know, and the words make sense. If you want to remember information, it
has to make sense. It also has to mean something to you. You remember things that are important to you.
For example, you may remember *Mississippi* because it is one of the 50 states, because someone you
know lives there, because it is famous for its riverboats, or just because it is fun to spell.

New Learning

 Even if information makes sense and has meaning for us, it can still drop out. Look at the clock. The
time on the clock says 18:24, but that isn't a time you normally see on a clock. The clock reminds us that
information must be practiced from 18 to 24 hours after it is presented. If you get new information on
Monday, practice it on Tuesday, and practice it again on Wednesday, the information has a better chance
of going into your long-term memory. Use any crayon to color the clock, and then use your green crayon
to trace the arrows showing that the new learning has made it to the long-term memory and has been
officially learned. If you are introduced to something new on Monday and don't practice it on Tuesday or
Wednesday, what is going to happen to that new information? (*Pause for answer.*) It is going to fall out.
Use your red crayon to trace the arrow that shows that the new information may not be learned.

Long-Term Memory (Storage)

You have finally made it to the last kind of memory. This is your long-term memory. Long-term memory is like a file cabinet. Learned information is stored there. When you have to remember something for a test, or a teacher asks you a question, the information you need to find is in your long-term memory. Use your blue crayon to color the file cabinet to show that learned information is stored in your brain. Sometimes it takes a little bit of time for the brain to find, or retrieve, the information to answer the question. That's why you might need a little bit of "wait time" before you can answer a question. But no matter what, since the information made it all the way to your long-term memory, you will be able to remember it, or retrieve it, to answer the question. Use your blue crayon to trace the curved line at the bottom of the file cabinet that represents your long-term memory. That shows that you are able to remember, or retrieve, information and then use it.

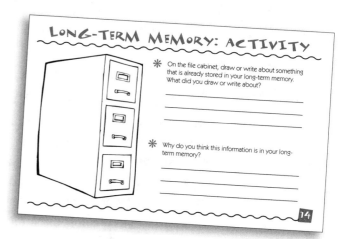

My Brain Booklet, page 14

(See reproducible page 40)

On page 14, you see a picture of a file cabinet from the side. This file cabinet represents your long-term memory. On the file cabinet, draw or write something that is already in your long-term memory. It can be a word you know how to spell, a special memory, directions for how to get to a place, or even a phone number. Then answer the questions next to the file cabinet.

Session * 4: This Is How I Remember

My Brain Booklet, page 15
(See reproducible page 41)

Let's take a look at what you have learned about your brain. First, information enters your brain through your five s____ (senses). *(As you read, have students fill in the correct words orally. Supply the first sound of each answer—this is a strategy on the Strategies Bookmark on page 13.)* If it is important to you, it goes through a filter that looks like window b____ (blinds). If it isn't important to you, the filter stays closed and the information drops o____ (out). Next, the information moves to your short-term memory. This is where the information must grab the brain's a____ (attention). By using color or pictures, music, movement, humor, or something new, the information is more interesting to your b____ (brain). If you try learning the information in different w___ (ways), it will be even easier. Then the information passes to the working memory which acts like a d____ (desk). Here you have to work with the information. You have to make it smaller by ch____ (chunking) it together into smaller pieces, then you have to pr____ (practice) it or the information will f____ (fall) out. The information has to make s____ (sense) to you and have m____ (meaning) if it is going to be r____ (remembered). You have to practice the information at a later time or the next d____ (day). If you do practice it 18 to 24 hours later, the information finally moves into your long-term m____ (memory). The information has been learned and your brain will store it here until you need to r____ (remember) it.

The brain helps you learn everything you know, but the brain can only learn if you do your part. You won't learn if you don't work at it. Let's review what you have to do to make sure information is learned. *(Review page 15 of the booklet with students.)*

My Brain Booklet, page 16
(See reproducible page 41)

Read the sentences on page 16 of your *My Brain Booklet*. See if you can unscramble the words to help you practice what you have learned about the brain. (If this activity is too difficult for students, allow them to work with a partner or do as a whole-group activity.) Next time, we will talk about your role—and mine—in the learning process.

Session #5: What Can I Do?

My Brain Booklet, page 17
(See reproducible page 42)

Your brain wants to learn. Do you? You found out how information flows through the brain and how it can fall out and not be remembered. Your job is to make sure that the information you are learning makes it to your long-term memory. Since music catches your brain's attention, let's do some singing to practice what you have learned.

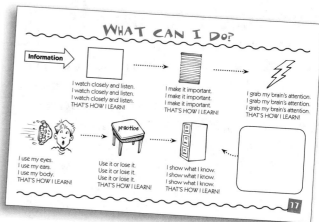

(As you review page 17 of the booklet with students, sing each step with them using the tune "Did You Ever See a Lassie?") You learned that the senses take in everything around us. In the box beside the arrow, draw your five senses (eyes, ears, nose, mouth, and hand). *(Begin singing and invite students to join in.)*

> *I watch closely and listen. I watch closely and listen. I watch closely and listen.*
> *That's how I learn.*

Next, the information goes to the filter that works like window blinds. If the information is important, the blinds open and the information passes through. If you don't think the information is important, the blinds close and the information drops out. So your attitude about learning matters, because you decide what is important. If you want to learn, then the information will be important to you. Color the blinds yellow to show light coming through. *(Begin singing the next verse and invite students to join in.)*

> *I make it important. I make it important. I make it important.*
> *That's how I learn.*

Now that the information has made it through the filter, where does it go?
(Pause for answers.) It goes to your short-term memory. If the information grabs your attention through color, music, movement, humor, or because it is new, you remember it. In the space next to the flash, draw a picture of yourself paying attention. *(Begin singing the next verse and invite students to join in.)*

> *I grab my brain's attention. I grab my brain's attention. I grab my brain's attention.*
> *That's how I learn.*

If you use more than one learning style (seeing, hearing, moving) to help you remember information, that can also help the short-term memory move it along. Sway back and forth while we sing this verse. *(Begin singing the next verse and invite students to join in.)*

> *I use my eyes. I use my ears. I use my body.*
> *That's how I learn.*

Once the information leaves your short-term memory, where does it go? *(Pause for answers.)* It goes to the working memory. The working memory is like a desk because you do the work (chunking and practicing) to keep information in your working memory. On the desk, circle the word *practice*. *(Begin singing the next verse of the song.)*

> Use it or lose it. Use it or lose it. Use it or lose it.
> That's how I learn.

After you practice the information for a day or two, where does it go? *(Pause for answers.)* It moves into your long-term memory, where it is stored until you need it. In the box next to the file cabinet, draw a person raising his or her hand to show that the person can retrieve the information from the "file cabinet." *(Begin the last verse of the song.)*

> I show what I know. I show what I know. I show what I know.
> That's how I learn.

My Brain Booklet, page 18

(See reproducible page 42)

In the first circle on page 18 of your booklet, draw your face and write the word *me* under it. In the second circle, draw a picture of a globe and write *my world* under it. In the third circle, draw a picture of a clock and write the word *time* under it. This will help you remember that you can remember information more easily if it means something to you, if it relates to your world and your life, and if you practice it before 18 to 24 hours have passed.

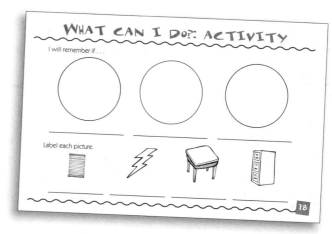

Last, label the four pictures at the bottom. *(Students should label the pictures **filter, short-term memory, working memory,** and **long-term memory**.)*

Session #5 (cont.): What I Will Do

My Brain Booklet, page 19
(See reproducible page 43)

You have spent a lot of time learning how the brain works. You have seen how information can pass through your memory or drop out. You also sang a song about what you need to do to help learning take place. You saw that teachers can help you learn by using color and pictures, song, movement, humor, and interesting ideas, and by helping you use several different ways to learn. Teachers can also help by making time for you to practice what you are learning.

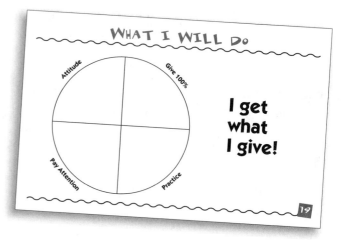

So, as a student, what will YOU do to help yourself learn? Your *attitude*—how you act, what you think about learning, and how you feel about yourself—will determine whether you learn or not. If you say *I don't want to do this* or *This is stupid* or *I can't do this* or *This is too hard,* you tell your brain not to learn. But if you have a positive attitude and want to learn, you will. *(Have a student come to the overhead and draw two self-portraits in the section labeled "Have a positive attitude." One should have a bad attitude and the other a good attitude. Have him or her cross out the picture with the bad attitude.)* The more you practice learning, the easier it will get. *(While the student is drawing at the overhead, make sure the rest are drawing on the diagrams in their booklets.)*

(Have one student come to the overhead and draw a picture of someone working hard—putting a lot of effort into something.) Effort means how hard you try. If you only work a little, say 20%, you'll only learn 20%. If you give 100%, it will be easier to learn 100%.

(Have another student come to the overhead and draw a picture of him- or herself paying attention in the section labeled "Pay Attention.") Next, you have to pay attention. It is your job to listen and think about what you are learning. If the information never makes it inside your brain, are you going to learn it?

(Circle Practice *in the last section.)* Once the information is in your brain, what do you have to do? *(Pause.)* "Practice" means doing something many times. Remember, if you don't use it, you lose it. *(Erase the drawings from the transparency.)*

Now, I want you to think about what you will do to help yourself learn. When you are finished, we will share the work. Look at the right side of the page and read what it says. It says *I get what I give.* What does that mean? If you give only a small amount, what will you get? If you give a large amount, what will you get? It's up to you. If you only give a little effort and time, don't work hard, and don't try your very best, you're only going to get a little out of it. But if you give your all, do all of the work, and put forth your best effort, you're going to get the most out of it. Let's say it all together: *I get what I give!*

My Brain Booklet, page 20

(See reproducible page 43)

This is the last page of your booklet. After this page, you are ready to begin using the information to improve your reading and learning. You can draw or write anything you want, as long as it has to do with what you have learned. Maybe you will write about how you want to use the information to improve your learning. Maybe you want to draw a picture to help you remember something that you learned about the brain and memory. Whatever you choose, be sure to draw or write something that will inspire you to do your best when you look back at this booklet.

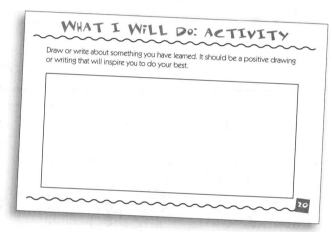

MY BRAIN

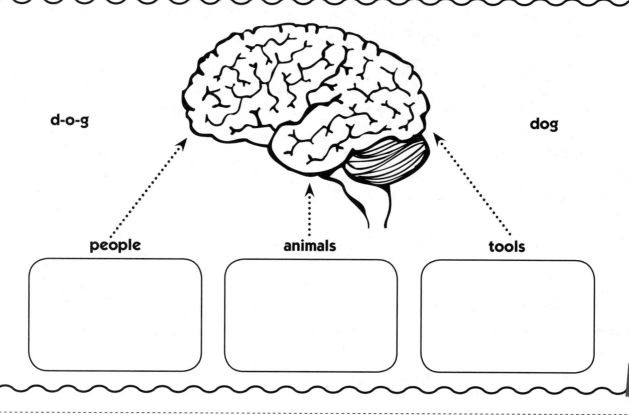

d-o-g

dog

people   animals   tools

1

MY BRAIN: ACTIVITY

✳ What does the brain look like to you?

_____

_____

_____

✳ Draw a picture of the brain. Why do
you think you are drawing this picture?

_____

_____

_____

2

Strategies For Struggling Readers © 2007 Creative Teaching Press

FRONT BRAIN AND BACK BRAIN

When you use the **front** of your brain to read, it looks like this:

I g-o t-o J-e-f-f-e-r-s-o-n S-c-h-o-o-l i-n C-a-r-l-s-b-a-d. I-t i-s a c-o-o-l s-c-h-o-o-l.

M-y n-a-m-e i-s_____

Write your name with a hyphen between each letter.

When you use the **back** of the brain to read, it looks like this:

I go to Jefferson School in Carlsbad. It is a cool school.

My name is_____

Write your name like you usually do.

3

- -

FRONT BRAIN AND BACK BRAIN: ACTIVITY

Which person do you think is the faster reader?
Circle that person. Why do you think so?

1a.	I l-i-k-e t-o b-u-y m-y l-u-n-c-h o-n T-h-u-r-s-d-a-y-s.
1b.	I like to buy my lunch on Thursdays.

2a.	O-n T-h-u-r-s-d-a-y-s, w-e h-a-v-e c-h-e-e-s-e p-i-z-z-a.
2b.	On Thursdays, we have cheese pizza.

4

HOW THE BRAIN WORKS

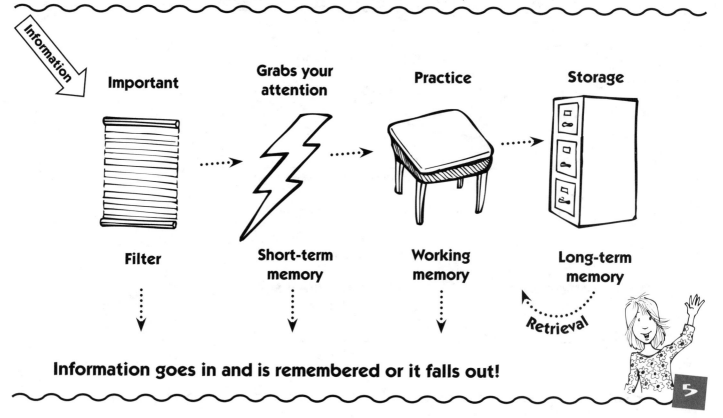

Information

Important   **Grabs your attention**   **Practice**   **Storage**

Filter   **Short-term memory**   **Working memory**   **Long-term memory**

Retrieval

Information goes in and is remembered or it falls out!

5

HOW THE BRAIN WORKS: ACTIVITY

Take an imaginary walk across the playground to see what your senses pick up. Draw or write about something you might see, hear, smell, and touch. Can you think of anything you might taste on the playground?

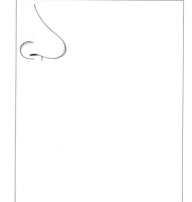

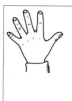

6

Strategies For Struggling Readers © 2007 Creative Teaching Press

SENSORY INPUT

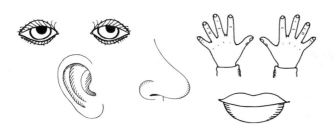

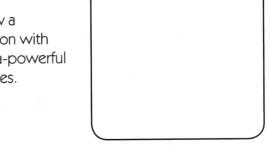

Draw a person with extra-powerful senses.

Information grabs your brain's attention when it's important.

Draw smoke.

Important information passes through the filter. If the information isn't important, it drops out.

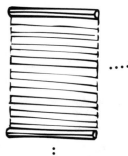

7

SENSORY INPUT: ACTIVITY

Close your fist. Look at each picture. If it is of something that interests you, open your fist. If it does not interest you, keep your fist closed. Circle the items that made you open your fist.

What made your filter open? Why? In the box, draw and color a picture of something else that would interest you.

8

SHORT-TERM MEMORY

These things help information move from your filter into your short-term memory.

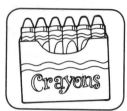

**pictures
and color**

**music
and rhythm**

movement

humor

new and different

**combining
learning styles**

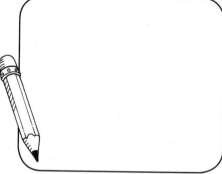

In the box, draw something interesting that you have learned about the brain.

9

SHORT-TERM MEMORY: ACTIVITY

In each set, circle the item or picture that you prefer.

a TV with a color picture

a black-and-white TV

saying multiplication tables

singing a math rap

clapping syllables

writing the number of syllables

a little red wagon

a magic carpet

10

Strategies For Struggling Readers © 2007 Creative Teaching Press

WORKING MEMORY

Working Memory can hold 5 things.

Chunking

9 3 8 6 4 2

M-i-s-s-i-s-s-i-p-p-i

[____ ____ ____   ]

[____ ____ ____ ____ ____   ]

Practice

Mississippi   Miss-iss-ipp-i

WORKING MEMORY: ACTIVITY

What can you do to help you remember
these groups of information?

Chunking
and
Practice

1 8 5 6 7 0   or   ____ ____ ____

2 1 4 3 8 6 9   or   _____ – _____

M-a-s-s-a-c-h-u-s-e-t-t-s   or   _____ _____ _____ _____

school   _____

story   _____

elephant   or   _____

banana   _____

trampoline   _____

LONG-TERM MEMORY

Information must **make sense** and have **meaning** to move to your long-term memory.

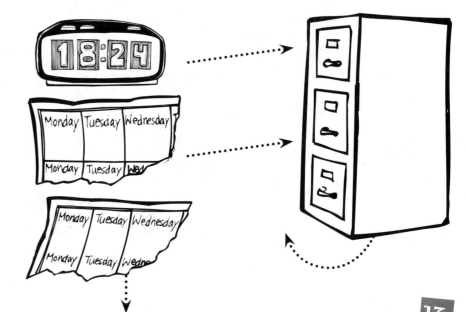

¢

hdstge
help me

Information must be **practiced** within 18 to 24 hours after it is learned to move to your long-term memory.

If information is not practiced, it will drop out.

LONG-TERM MEMORY: ACTIVITY

❋ On the file cabinet, draw or write about something that is already stored in your long-term memory. What did you draw or write about?

_____

_____

_____

❋ Why do you think this information is in your long-term memory?

_____

_____

_____

THIS IS HOW I REMEMBER

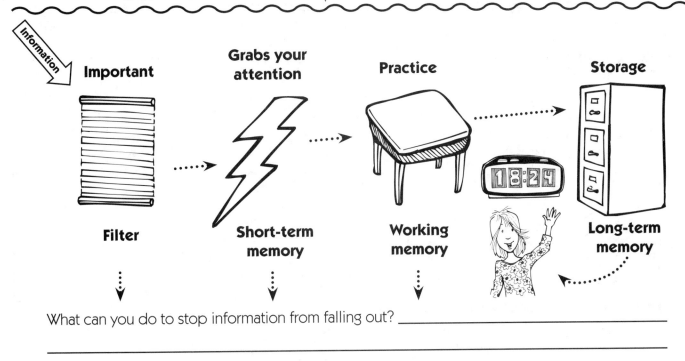

What can you do to stop information from falling out? _____

_____

_____

THIS IS HOW I REMEMBER: ACTIVITY

You can use your five *essnse* _____ to get information.

The information must be *ttimopran* _____ enough to pass through the filter.

Next, information moves to your *rotsh-ermt* _____ memory.

Information then moves to your *krongwi* _____ memory.

To keep memory from falling out at this point, you need to *hunck* _____ information and *racipcet* _____.

If you work with the information within 18 to 24 hours after you learn it, it moves into your *glon-mert* _____ memory.

Congratulations! You can now *teiverre* _____ the information any time you need it.

WHAT CAN I DO?

Information → 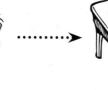 ┈┈► ┈┈►

I watch closely and listen.
I watch closely and listen.
I watch closely and listen.
THAT'S HOW I LEARN!

I make it important.
I make it important.
I make it important.
THAT'S HOW I LEARN!

I grab my brain's attention.
I grab my brain's attention.
I grab my brain's attention.
THAT'S HOW I LEARN!

 ┈┈► 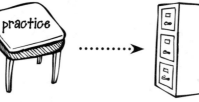 ┈┈►  ◄┈┈

I use my eyes.
I use my ears.
I use my body.
THAT'S HOW I LEARN!

Use it or lose it.
Use it or lose it.
Use it or lose it.
THAT'S HOW I LEARN!

I show what I know.
I show what I know.
I show what I know.
THAT'S HOW I LEARN!

17

WHAT CAN I DO?: ACTIVITY

I will remember if . . .

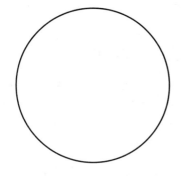   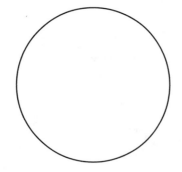   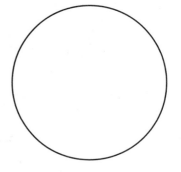

_____   _____   _____

Label each picture.

_____   _____   _____   _____

18

WHAT I WILL DO

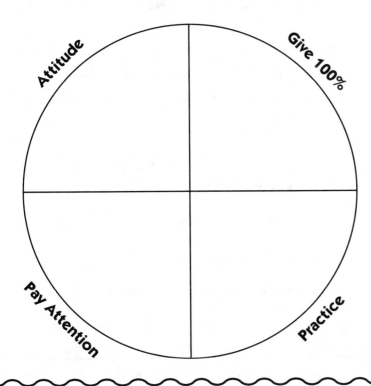

Attitude

Give 100%

Pay Attention

Practice

I get what I give!

<sub>

</sub>

WHAT I WILL DO: ACTIVITY

Draw or write about something you have learned. It should be a positive drawing or writing that will inspire you to do your best.

Reading Activities Overview

Now that students are familiar with how their brains work, it is time to put that learning to good use while students focus on improving their reading. Here is a recap of the brain-based techniques students and teachers can implement to help build strong foundations in phonemic awareness, phonics, vocabulary, fluency, and comprehension:

- Use color and pictures, music and rhythm, movement, humor, and novel approaches to help their brains pay attention to new concepts.

- Employ two learning styles (auditory, visual, or kinesthetic) for each new concept.

- Practice new information at least twice within 18 to 24 hours.

- Frequently discuss student progress and attitudes and teacher methods.

The next five sections provide background and activities related to the five components of reading: phonemic awareness, phonics, vocabulary and word recognition, fluency, and comprehension. The activities address each component individually and provide support to help students strengthen these skill areas.

Each reading activity consists of these parts:
* **Objectives:** Tell the purpose of the activity. Share this information as part of the attitude, progress, and method discussions (above).

 Brain-based learning elements: Explain what research findings and brain-based techniques are used in each activity. Share this information with students, as well.

 Directions: Step-by-step instructions for completing each activity.

Extensions: Any additional related activities that reinforce concepts.

Students will complete many reproducible activities in pairs or groups, or with you modeling them on a transparency. To give students further practice without making many more reproducibles, laminate a few additional copies and store them with erasable markers. Allow students to work on them independently.

Phonemic Awareness

The aim of phonemic awareness is to help children develop an ear for language—to hear specific sounds, identify sound sequences, and understand the role phonemes (sounds) play in word formation. Phonological awareness is sequential, beginning with the awareness of spoken words, then syllables, then onsets and rimes, and finally individual sounds within words (phonemic awareness). Before students can identify a letter that stands for a sound, they must be able to hear that individual sound in a word. This is difficult because sounds are abstract in nature, but being aware of sound differences in spoken language is crucial when learning to read written language.

Prerequisite Skills in Phonemic Awareness

In order to build a strong foundation in reading, at-risk readers must do the following:

- Have phonological awareness—the awareness that language can be broken into smaller components (sentences into words, words into syllables, syllables into sounds).

- Demonstrate an understanding of onsets and rimes and rhyming words.

- Identify beginning, medial, and ending sounds.

- Approximate sounds (identify positions of given sounds).

- Segment words into individual phonemes (/c/ /a/ /t/).

- Add, delete, and change sounds to make new words.

- Recognize that letters represent sounds (the alphabetic principle).

Recommendations

While older students have often had exposure to reading, some may not have had the adequate training needed to develop their phonological skills. Practice with phonemic awareness concepts will help them build new neural circuits. Using brain-based learning techniques and explaining the *whys* of activities will provide practice, heighten interest, and help to make "remedial" activities acceptable to older students.

Rhyming Riddles (Hinky Pinks)

* EXPOSE STUDENTS TO ONSETS AND RIMES THROUGH RHYMING WORD PAIRS.

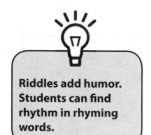

Riddles add humor. Students can find rhythm in rhyming words.

 **Directions** Read the riddles below.
Encourage students to guess the answers.

What do you call a . . .

chubby kitten?	→	(fat cat)
crying father?	→	(sad dad)
silly rabbit?	→	(funny bunny)
huge hog?	→	(big pig)
tidy road?	→	(neat street)

reptile's dessert?	→	(snake's cake)
library corner?	→	(book nook)
colorful mattress?	→	(red bed)
overweight rodent?	→	(fat rat)
meat burglar?	→	(beef thief)

Students should quickly notice that all answers are rhyming pairs. Discuss the criteria for rhyming words. Students might say that rhyming words sound and look alike. Invite students to brainstorm a list of rhyming words. Write them on the board. Point out similar rimes in words, such as *ew* in *new* and *stew*. Write an irregular rhyming word, such as *shoe*. Guide the discussion until students recognize that rhyming words must have the same sounds but can be spelled in different ways.

Auditory Match-Up

* TEACH STUDENTS TO IDENTIFY BEGINNING AND ENDING PHONEMES.

Play a game to catch students' attention.

 **Directions** Divide the class into a beginning sound team and an ending sound team. Choose and say a key word from the **Multisyllable Word List (page 49)**. Have the first member of the beginning sound team say a word that begins with the same sound as the key word. Have the first member of the ending sound team say a word that begins with the ending sound of the key word. For example, if the key word is *snail*, the beginning sound team member might say *seal* and the ending sound team member might say *lion*. Switch team designations so that all students practice beginning and ending sounds.

Extension: Have students identify the medial sounds in key words and say other words that have the same medial sounds. For example, if the key word is *met*, one team member might say *beg* and another might say *pen*. Do not let students use rhyming words for their responses, since the emphasis will fall on the rimes rather than the vowel sounds.

Phonological Coding

* TEACH STUDENTS TO BLEND PHONEMES (COMBINE SOUNDS) TO IDENTIFY WORDS.

Students will use pictures for this activity.

 **Directions** ►

Explain that putting sounds together to make words or breaking apart sounds in words takes place in the phonological part of the brain. This part of the brain identifies words before determining pronunciation, spelling, and meaning. Practicing with sounds and words reinforces this ability. Have students listen as you orally segment a word. For example, say *jump*, but pause between each sound /j/, /u/, /m/, /p/. Invite them to combine the sounds, identify the word, and say *jump*. Repeat with other two-, three-, four-, and five-phoneme words (listed below):

2 phonemes	3 phonemes	4 phonemes	5 phonemes
pie /p/, /i/	bat /b/, /a/, /t/	stars /s/, /t/, /ar/, /s/	zebra /z/, /e/, /b/, /r/, /a/
toe /t/, /o/	boat /b/, /o/, /t/	lamp /l/, /a/, /m/, /p/	robot /r/, /o/, /b/, /o/, /t/
tea /t/, /e/	ball /b/, /a/, /l/	turtle /t/, /r/, /t/, /l/	peanut /p/, /e/, /n/, /u/, /t/
key /k/, /e/	fish /f/, /i/, /sh/	tiger /t/, /i/, /g/, /r/	puppet /p/, /u/, /p/, /e/, /t/

Then let students cut apart copies of the **Phoneme Picture Cards (pages 50–51)** and sort the pictures by the number of phonemes they contain.

Phoneme Sort

* TEACH STUDENTS TO SEGMENT WORDS INTO INDIVIDUAL SOUNDS (PHONEMES).

Using nonsense words adds novelty, while counters add a kinesthetic element.

 **Directions** ►

Discuss how the brain breaks words into individual sounds. Reinforce how important this skill is in reading and spelling. Explain that this skill is called segmenting.

Give each student a copy of the **Phoneme Graph reproducible (page 52)** and five counters (dried beans or pennies). Say a word from the **Nonsense Word List (page 53).** (All nonsense words listed have short vowels.) Tell students to repeat each nonsense word, count the number of sounds, and place a counter above the corresponding number on the graph. For example, say the nonsense word *muz*. Students should repeat the word, determine that it has three sounds, and place a counter above the 3 on the graph.

> Phoneme Graph
>
> | | | | |
> |---|---|---|---|
> | | | | |
> | | 🪙 | | |
> | 🪙 | 🪙 | | 🪙 |
> | 🪙 | 🪙 | 🪙 | 🪙 |
> | 2 | 3 | 4 | 5 |

Note that in some words, two letters represent one sound. For example, there are four letters in boat but only three sounds. When segmenting oral words and counting the number of sounds, students (especially those who have had extensive experience with printed words and text) have a tendency to visualize the word and count the number of letters (graphemes) rather than the number of sounds (phonemes). Nonsense words help students avoid this tendency. Students have not seen nonsense words in print and will have an easier time counting just the sounds.

Sound Manipulation

* HELP STUDENTS CREATE NEW WORDS BY MANIPULATING SOUNDS WITHIN WORDS.

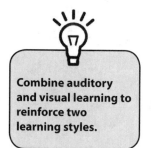

Combine auditory and visual learning to reinforce two learning styles.

Explain that *manipulate* means *move around*. Say a one-syllable word from the **Multisyllable Word List (page 49)**, give a direction to change the word, and have students say the new word. For example, say *pan*. Tell students to change the *n* to a *t* to make *pat*, then change the *p* to a *b* to make *bat*, then change the *t* to a *th* to make *bath*. While this is an auditory activity, writing the words may help students better understand the lesson. Once students seem comfortable with the manipulation, only give the words orally. As students become competent at changing letters, have them drop letters from words and determine the new words. For example, say *nest*. Ask students to drop the letter *s* (net). Say *tent*. Ask students to drop the final *t* (ten). Say *stomp*. Ask students to drop the letter *m* (stop).

Extension: Have students change vowel sounds rather than consonant sounds. When using short vowel words, say the vowel *sound* rather than the letter name. For example, Say the word *not*. Change the /o/ to /u/. Students should answer that this makes *nut*.

Change It!

* TEACH CHILDREN TO CREATE NEW WORDS BY MANIPULATING PHONEMES WITHIN EXISTING WORDS.

Playing a game and the movement of using a spinner add interest.

Copy, cut out, laminate, and assemble a **Change It Spinner (page 54)**. Say a one-syllable word from the **Multisyllable Word List (page 49)**.

Invite a student to spin the Change-It Spinner. If the spinner lands on *Beginning*, ask the student to change the first sound of the word to make a new word. If the spinner lands on *End*, invite the student to change the last sound to make a new word. If the spinner lands on *Middle*, have the student change the vowel. Have students take turns spinning the spinner for each one-syllable word you say aloud.

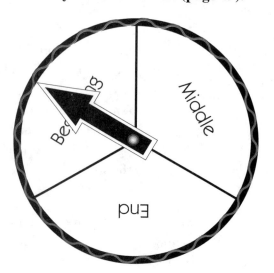

Multisyllable Word List

One-Syllable Words

beach	cake	cup	gum	net	plate	tent
bear	clock	dish	hand	nose	snail	train
bread	cloud	drum	hat	nut	sled	
bridge	corn	flag	lamp	pan	stick	
broom	crib	foot	leg	plant	tape	

Two-Syllable Words

airplane	carrot	finger	monkey	rabbit	tractor
apple	circus	fireplace	paper	rainbow	zebra
baby	cowboy	glasses	pizza	spider	
baseball	dolphin	kitten	popcorn	starfish	
basket	elbow	lemon	pumpkin	table	
camel	faucet	lettuce	puppet	tiger	

Three-Syllable Words

animal	crocodile	hamburger	parachute	submarine	underground
astronaut	decorate	icicle	porcupine	sunglasses	valentine
banana	dinosaur	jellyfish	potato	telescope	
basketball	dishwasher	kangaroo	radio	tomato	
bicycle	elephant	lollipop	screwdriver	tricycle	
computer	grandmother	magician	spaghetti	umbrella	

Four-Syllable Words

alligator	dictionary	harmonica	invisible	responsible	television
apologize	elevator	helicopter	motorcycle	ridiculous	thermometer
calculator	escalator	hibernation	mysterious	stegosaurus	triceratops
caterpillar	experiment	information	pepperoni	supermarket	watermelon

Five-Syllable Words

cafeteria	condominium	hippopotamus	refrigerator
certification	electricity	pronunciation	

Phoneme Picture Cards

Phoneme Picture Cards

4		
5		

Phoneme Graph

2	**3**	**4**	**5**

Nonsense Word List

Two Phonemes

zo	ve	che	tho	za
fi	sho	shu	fo	ge
pu	thu	chu	be	
ca	wha	shi	wi	

Three Phonemes

zaf	mof	miz	thim	whez
veb	huj	wov	wom	thab
pid	fap	shaz	chag	shil
muz	pef	choz	shup	

Four Phonemes

slup	smit	snad	blav	crog
grap	glab	grep	bris	scaz
drit	skif	glin	clud	chib
snef	cloj	smub	glef	

Five Phonemes

slonk	morst	snabl	trimd	snult
clant	skinf	clonk	stald	clist
drist	glist	smuld	bleft	drorv
gronk	snust	stilf	srast	

Change It Spinner

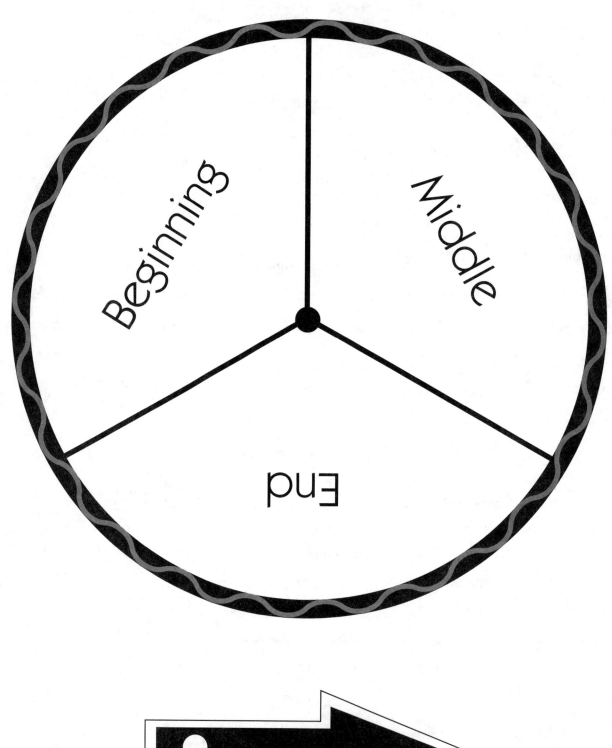

Phonics

Phonics is an instructional approach for teaching reading and spelling that emphasizes sound-symbol relationships. It is based on the alphabetic principle: spoken words are made up of sounds (phonemes), and these sounds are represented by letters (graphemes). Phonics instruction should be sequential, with one skill building on another. However, many struggling readers' phonics instruction has been haphazard, leaving students confused and overwhelmed. They find that the dual task of decoding and comprehending requires more energy and attention than is available. To compensate, struggling readers employ a "divide and conquer" strategy, decoding words first and then switching to comprehension. By alternating, struggling readers can work through text, but progress is slow and difficult. Starting over with an accelerated, implicit word-attack program can quickly provide students with a solid foundation that will allow them to develop skills to decode text and comprehend the words that they read. Once students understand the alphabetic principle, the task of decoding words becomes automatic, allowing students to use all of their energy on comprehension (back-brain reading).

Prerequisite Skills in Phonemic Awareness

To have a strong foundation in phonics, at-risk readers need to do the following:

- Gain a working knowledge of the alphabetic principle.
- Discriminate between short vowel sounds and read short vowel words.
- Automatically blend sounds into words (CVC-CCVC-CVCC).
- Identify long vowel spellings and rules.
- Orally change vowel sounds in words.
- Identify vowel combinations and their sounds.
- Become familiar with irregular spelling patterns.
- Read multisyllabic words.
- Identify root words and affixes.

Recommendations

First, use a diagnostic and oral reading inventory to assess students' decoding skills. Next, use a test that has students decode basic phonetic elements. Struggling readers can often decode short- and long-vowel words, but they do not know sounds or vowel spellings in isolation. This becomes a problem when they attempt to decode unfamiliar or multisyllabic words. Work and assessment with nonsense words is a good way to determine if students know the phonetic elements and can process them to make words.

Short Vowel Song

* IMPROVE STUDENTS' RETENTION OF SHORT VOWEL SOUNDS.

Using music, rhythm, and movement, and incorporating pictures, will move short vowel sounds into students' working memories.

 **Directions** → Give each student a copy of the **Short Vowel Picture Prompts reproducible (page 68)** and have students cut apart the cards. (Store cards in plastic bags for future use.) As you show the picture cards, have students join you in singing the song and making the gestures (below). Remind students that singing is not "baby stuff," because it activates the brain and improves learning. (Believe it or not, even most older kids will participate and like it!)

Short Vowel Song

(Tune: "The Mockingbird Song" also known as "Hush Little Baby")

/a/ /a/ /a/ /a/ /a/ /a/ /a/
Pet the lamb, short a says /a/.
(Curve left hand and pet with right hand.)

/e/ /e/ /e/ /e/ /e/ /e/ /e/
Grandpa Ed can't hear, short e says /e/.
(Put hand to ear and bob head as you sing.)

/i/ /i/ /i/ /i/ /i/ /i/ /i/
Icky pig, short i says /i/.
(Wrinkle up nose and hold it with fingers.)

/o/ /o/ /o/ /o/ /o/ /o/ /o/
Open wide, short o says /o/.
(Place finger on lip like a doctor's tongue depressor.)

/u/ /u/ /u/ /u/ /u/ /u/ /u/
Bear cub in the mud, short u says /u/.
(Make fists, round off shoulders, and move from side to side.)

After the students have been introduced to the picture prompts and song, pass out picture sets to each student and have them hold up the appropriate picture card as they sing. This combines the visual (pictures), the auditory, (song), and the kinesthetic (movement) modalities.

Extension: Sing the song by yourself. As you reach the *short _ says / _ /* portion of each verse, do not sing the vowel sound, but let students hold up the appropriate cards.

Short Vowel Response Cards

* HELP STUDENTS IDENTIFY BEGINNING AND MEDIAL SHORT VOWEL SOUNDS IN WORDS.

Using humor (hiccups) helps student remember information.

 **Directions** ▶ Review the **"Short Vowel Song" (page 56)**. Give each student a set of **Short Vowel Picture Prompts (page 68)** from the previous activity. Have students place the cards in a row. Say each short vowel sound. Invite students to repeat the sounds and hold up the appropriate cards. Next, switch from using sounds to words. Tell students to listen to each word, repeat it, and hold up the card that represents the short vowel sound. (Initially, use words from the **Short Vowel Word Lists—One-Syllable Words, page 69, and Consonant Blends and Digraphs, page 70**—that begin with short vowel sounds. Then move to words with short vowel sounds in the middle.) If students have difficulty hearing the medial vowels, teach them how to use "hiccups" to emphasize the sound. Say the beginning of the word, exaggerating the vowel sound by saying it three times. Then finish saying the word. For example, for the word *man*, say *m... a...a... a...an.*

Extension: As students begin to easily identify the vowel sounds, use words from the **Short Vowel Word Lists (page 69–70)** that have initial blends or digraphs.

Short Vowel Sorting

* HELP STUDENTS IDENTIFY AND DISCRIMINATE BETWEEN SHORT VOWEL SOUNDS IN WORDS.

Explain again that the brain must break down words into sounds. To make this automatic, the brain must instantly connect letters and sounds to recognize words. The more students practice, the quicker the brain can read words. Playing a game is a fun way to practice.

 **Directions** ▶ Give each student a **Vowel-O Game Board (page 71)**. Have students circle the vowel over the column that they think will fill up first. Say a word from the **Short Vowel Word Lists (pages 69–70)**. As you say a word, students should write it in the appropriate vowel-sound column. When students fill up a column, students who circled that letter on their papers should call out *Vowel-O!* Play until all columns are filled.

Extension: Let each student choose a short vowel **letter tile** (a, e, i, o, u) from a **grab bag**, and program a Vowel-O Game Board by writing a word containing that vowel sound in the appropriate box. (To increase the difficulty, specify how many letters the word must have.) When the game boards are full, have students read their words to their partners.

Name _Holly_

Vowel-O Game Board

a	e	i	o	ⓤ
man	jet	hip	mop	nut
hat	yes		job	run
bad			fox	cup
pal				mud

Short Vowel Sound Puzzle

* TEACH STUDENTS TO IDENTIFY SHORT VOWEL SOUNDS.

Combine learning styles for better learning.

 **Directions** ➤ Distribute a **Short Vowel Sound Puzzle (page 73)** to each student. As you say a one-syllable word from the **Short Vowel Word Lists (pages 69–70)**, tell students to decide which short vowel sound they hear in that word. Pause after saying each word to let students identify the correct vowel sound. If they are not sure, remind them to use the "hiccups" strategy (/f/, /l/, /a/, /a/, /a/, /at/). If necessary, repeat the word, emphasizing the short vowel sound. Invite each student pair to use **crayons** or **markers** to color a section of the appropriate vowel. After you have repeated all of the words, have student pairs record their findings on a graph. Discuss the results.

Short Vowel Flashcards

* HELP STUDENTS BUILD AUTOMATIC RECOGNITION OF SHORT VOWEL SOUNDS AND WORDS.

Use color to increase vowel recognition automaticity.

 **Directions** ➤ Write words from the **Short Vowel Word Lists (page 69–70)** on **index cards**. Write the consonants in black and the vowels in red. Shuffle the cards. Remind students that color grabs the brain's attention and that using two different colors is ideal. Tell students that they are going to help the brain process words quickly by first identifying the vowel sounds in those words. As you show students the flash cards, tell them to read only the red part, not the entire word. Illustrate by showing the cards slowly and saying only the vowel sounds. Have students join in. Increase the speed with which you show the cards until it is so fast that students cannot identify the vowel sounds. Explain that with daily practice, their brains will learn to process the information more quickly and they will soon be able to read the vowel sounds at a rapid pace. When this happens, the brain's recognition process has become automatic.

Once students can quickly identify the vowel sounds, have them say the vowel sounds and then the words. Initially, they will say each vowel sound then pause before they read the word. Have students practice until the pause is eliminated. Point out that students no longer pause because the brain has developed automaticity, or automatic recognition.

Making and Writing Words

*HELP STUDENTS IDENTIFY AND DISTINGUISH SHORT VOWEL SOUNDS IN WORDS.

Directions ➤ Select a word related to a story theme or that contains the phonetic elements you wish to emphasize (such as words with CVC and a blend). In random order, write the vowels and consonants in the appropriate boxes on a **transparency** of the **Making and Writing Words reproducible (page 74)**. For example, if the word is *spider*, write *i* and *e* in the vowels box and *d, s, r, p* in the consonant box. Show students the transparency and tell them to use the letters on it to make new words. Allow them to call out words for you to record. When they have finished making as many smaller words as they can, encourage them to make a single word using all of the letters at once. When students are ready, let them do the activity independently.

Using a graphic organizer (visual learning) and riddles (novelty) helps students pay close attention and remember the lesson.

Extension: Use the lower boxes of the reproducible for a spelling activity related to word meaning. In advance, write a list of words that can be made using the letters in the top two boxes. Create a clue for each word, such as *what water does when a faucet is leaky* (drip). Invite students to spell a word that fits the clue and record it in a word box on the transparency. As students' skills improve, let them complete this activity independently or in pairs. Eventually, students may even be able to write their own clues.

Word Swap

*HELP STUDENTS MANIPULATE SOUNDS IN THE INITIAL, MEDIAL, AND END POSITIONS IN WORDS.

Directions ➤ Distribute copies of the **Word Swap reproducible (page 75)**. Choose a key word from the **Word Line Word List (page 72)**, and demonstrate how to change its beginning sound. Write the new word in the first box on the Word Swap reproducible. In the next box, have students change the ending sounds, write the new words, and then read them aloud. In the last box, demonstrate how to change the middle sound by adding a different short vowel sound. Remind students that when changing the vowel sound they may end up making nonsense words. While this gives good practice in blending words, use only real words for this activity. Have students read the new words they created by manipulating the sounds.

Changing and manipulating letters improves decoding skills.

Finally, introduce the Bonus Words section. Tell students that they will use the last word in each of the three sections to make new words, but this time they should change two letters as designated.

Little Words in Big

*SHOW STUDENTS HOW TO FURTHER IMPROVE THEIR DECODING SKILLS USING SPECIFIC STRATEGIES.

Using colored markings helps students "chunk" and see letter patterns, which increases decoding speed.

 Write a few words from the **Word Hunt reproducible (page 76)** on the board. Have students read the words. Ask *how* they were able to read the words. Invite students to be detectives and find the clues that helped them identify the words. As students discover that there are little words inside each of the big words, draw a blue box around each little word. (If students do not notice this, put blue boxes around the little words and wait for students to realize what you are doing.) Explain that they should be able to hear the little words inside of the big words. For example, they can hear the word *other* in the word *another*, but even though they can see the word *her,* they cannot hear it. Point to each word and say *little word*. After students read a little word, say *big word*, and have students read the big word.

Give each student a Word Hunt reproducible and a **blue pencil**. Tell students to look at the list of words and draw a blue box around any little words in a bigger word. Remind students that the brain is attracted to color and that the blue pencils will make the little words stand out. Have them quietly read each little word and then the bigger word as they are drawing blue boxes. When students have finished, ask them to read all of the words together, first identifying the little word and then the bigger one.

Syllable Spot

*TEACH STUDENTS TO DECODE MULTISYLLABLE WORDS.

Writing the words in color will help students focus on them. In the extension, letting students choose words and using their words for another session of this activity (held within 18-24 hours) will give appropriately timed practice.

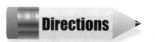 Write some words from the **Multisyllable Word List (page 49)** on the board, using a dot to divide each syllable. Write the words in a bright color and the dots in black (white if using a chalkboard). (Make a "cheat sheet" of the words you select since you will be erasing them and rewriting them in a different order.) Have students read each word aloud syllable by syllable and then as a whole word. Erase the words and rewrite them in a different order as whole words. Ask students to read the whole words as quickly as possible. Then have students look at each word and say the number of syllables the word contains. Explain that spotting syllables in words will make it easier to decode and read longer words.

What Makes Long Vowels Long?

* IMPROVE STUDENTS' RECOGNITION AND AUTOMATICITY OF LONG VOWEL WORD SPELLINGS.

 **Directions**

Select words from the **Long Vowel Word List (page 78)**. Choose words with signal *e* (CVCE), such as *hike*, and with two-letter long vowel spellings-called 2-fers", as in *oa* in *goat*. They are called "2-fers" because there are 2 letters for 1 sound. Use **index cards** to make flash cards of these words. Preselect five cards that have the signal *e* and five with two-letter long vowel spellings. Distribute a copy of the **What Makes Long Vowels Long? reproducible (page 79)** to each student. Explain that students need to learn to immediately spot signals and long-vowel spellings in words. Show the flash cards one at a time. Invite students to write tally marks in the appropriate boxes indicating whether the word has a signal *e* or a double vowel spelling. Note that reading the words is not part of the activity. The goal is to have students develop automatic recognition of the long vowel spellings. Once students are used to spotting the long vowel criteria, invite them to write the words on the What Makes Long Vowels Long? reproducible in the appropriate category and then read the words aloud. Make sure that

Students will use the same brain-based techniques as those that they used with their short vowel study, such as color, multiple learning styles, and hands-on (kinesthetic) activities to automatically recognize long vowel spellings.

students draw the arrow from the *signal e* to the long vowel, and add a bracket under the *"2-fers"*. (cake)   (goat)

Signal e Race

* HELP STUDENTS IMPROVE RECOGNITION OF SILENT E LONG VOWEL SPELLINGS.

Increasing speed will improve students' automaticity and back-brain reading.

 **Directions**

Use **index cards** to prepare flash cards that contain short vowel words and related long vowel words with a signal *e*, as in the following examples:

kit	kite	us	use
bit	bite	cap	cape
rat	rate	tub	tube
not	note	mop	mope

Explain that it is important for students to learn to immediately spot a signal *e* in a word. Tell them to make a continuous /s/ sound as you show a set of flash cards. When they see a signal *e* word, invite them to say *signal*. Initially, do not have students read the words because the goal is to achieve visual recognition of the signal *e*. Repeat the activity often for automaticity. Each time students do the activity, flip the cards faster until each word is seen for less than a second. When students can identify the signal *e*, have students read the words. Practice until students can easily read the words as you flip them quickly.

Extension: To reinforce signal *e* with color, prepare an additional flash card set. Use black ink to write consonants. Write the signal *e* and long vowels in red. As students learn to spot the red *e*, substitute a few cards at a time with the words written entirely in black ink.

Speedball Vowels

* GIVE STUDENTS FURTHER PRACTICE WITH IDENTIFYING LONG VOWEL SPELLINGS.

Using color helps students pay attention to the vowel spellings.

 **Directions** ▶ Use **index cards** to prepare flash cards for the long vowel sounds below. Use a different color for each of the five long vowel sounds. If possible, give a **whiteboard** to each student.

A	E	I	O	U
a_e	e_e	i_e	o_e	u_e
_ai_	_ea_	_igh	_oa_	_ew
_ay	__y	_y	_ow	

Explain that students will learn to see each two-letter pattern as one sound. Tell students that these are called *"2-fers"—two letters for one sound and remind them how the signal* e *works.* Explain to students that the blanks represent where letters go. Some vowel spellings are usually in the middle of a word (_ai_) and some at the end of a word (_ay). Ask students to look at the vowel spellings (highlighted in color) and say the vowel sounds as you flip through the flash cards. Increase the speed each time you flip through the cards.

As students demonstrate automatic recognition of the words, have them identify the vowel sound on each flash card. On their whiteboards, have them write another way of spelling each sound. For example, if a flash card shows long *a* as **ay,** students may write either **a_e** or **ai.**

Reading Links

* GIVE MORE PRACTICE IN RECOGNIZING LONG VOWEL SPELLINGS.

Having students write the words twice and then read them aloud will help reach visual, auditory, and kinesthetic learners. Having students complete the extension work within 24 hours of the initial exercise gives them appropriate practice.

 **Directions** ▶ Select long vowel spelling patterns from the **Long Vowel Word List (page 78)**. Write each spelling pattern on a separate, **interlocking cube**. Place each set of cubes in a small **plastic bag**. Pair students and give each pair a bag with a set of vowel cubes. Invite pairs to choose a cube and write a word that contains that vowel spelling. Have pairs continue until they have written a word for each cube. Then make a word graph using the vowel spellings. Have pairs add the words they made to the appropriate columns. When the graph is complete, have students read the words.

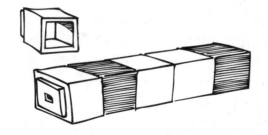

Switcheroo

* MOVE STUDENTS FROM JUST RECOGNIZING LONG VOWEL SPELLINGS TO THE MORE DIFFICULT SKILL OF SUBSTITUTING LETTERS TO MAKE NEW LONG VOWEL WORDS.

 On the board, demonstrate how one letter in a two-letter vowel pattern can be changed to make a new word, such as changing the word *beat* to *boat*. On the board, write some words from the list below. Invite students to work together to write all of the new words they can create by substituting one or more vowels.

Extra practice helps students read long vowel words automatically. Color-coding different vowels helps students pay attention to patterns.

Change 1 letter to make a new long vowel word:

bake (bike)	load (lead)	leaf (loaf)	space (spice)	like (Luke)
chose (chase)	blow (blew)	fume (fame)	lone (line)	wide (wade)
mule (mole)	road (read)	race (rice)	those (these)	mile (male)

Change 2 or more letters to make a new long vowel word:

gate (goat)	sheep (shape)	braid (bride)	fly (flew)	feel (fail)
wheat (white)	cry (crew)	life (loaf)	note (night)	bean (bone)
hail (hole)	toad (tide)	float (fleet)	seat (sight)	sweep (swipe)
bait (bite)	spike (speak)	froze (freeze)	seep (soap)	raid (ride)

Extension: When students are skilled at substituting letters, explain that sometimes changing a vowel sound is as simple as rearranging the vowels that are already in the word. Give them some practice with words from the list below, and then let students try to think of words that fit this pattern or circle them in their reading.

seal (sale)   eat (ate)   same (seam)   feat (fate)   heat (hate)

Word Sorts

* CONTINUE PRACTICING RECOGNIZING LONG VOWEL SPELLINGS.

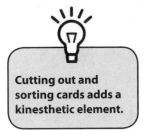

 Choose four long vowel word categories from the **Long Vowel Word List (page 78)** that you wish to reinforce. Write the four category names in the four blank boxes at the top of the **Word Cards reproducible (page 80)**. Write the selected words in the remaining boxes. Distribute a copy of the customized Word Card reproducible to each student. Have each student work with a partner to cut out the word cards and sort them according to their vowel spellings. When the partners have finished, ask them to read their words aloud. Invite partners to move to another group's word sort and read those words. Continue until students have read all of the word sorts. Explain that this type of practice (reading the same words over and over again) will help their brains quickly recognize the vowel sounds and result in faster word recognition.

Cutting out and sorting cards adds a kinesthetic element.

Long Vowel Classification

* MOVE STUDENTS FROM RECOGNIZING TO CLASSIFYING LONG VOWEL SOUNDS BY IDENTIFYING SPELLING PATTERNS.

Reading and writing (and marking the long vowel spellings in color) give students a number of modes in which to work on this skill. Practice time meets the requirements for ensuring long-term memory storage of long vowel patterns.

 **Directions** ➤ Select words from the **Long Vowel Word List (page 78)**. Choose words to represent both signal *e* and two-vowel combination spellings. Write a column of 10 words on the board. Discuss what makes vowels long, and then explain that these words will be easier to read once students' eyes and brains are trained to automatically see the signal *e* and the two vowels together. Ask students to read all of the words in 10 seconds as you time them using a **stopwatch**. Distribute copies of the **Long Vowel Classification reproducible (page 81)** to students, and then let them decide how to classify the words and write them under the appropriate headings.

Next, students should use **red pencils** to mark each signal *e* with an arrow and each two-letter vowel combination with a bracket. They should then quietly read the words independently. When all students are finished, let them try again to read all of the words in 30 seconds. Have them read the words a few more times. Each time, reduce the allotted time by five seconds. Repeat the activity with 10 new words each day of the week.

Add a Vowel

* SHOW STUDENTS HOW TO CHANGE SHORT VOWEL WORDS TO LONG VOWEL WORDS USING PREVIOUSLY IDENTIFIED LONG VOWEL SPELLING PATTERNS.

Using previously acquired skills in a new way grabs the brain's attention. Plus, since students are working together, they must read, write, and talk using different learning styles to accomplish the task.

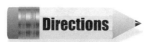 **Directions** ➤ Discuss what makes vowels long. Write the short vowel words *cot, fin, pan, set,* and *tub* on the board. Ask students to identify what kind of vowels are in these words (short). Ask students how they would change these short vowel words into long vowel words. Point to the word *cot* on the board, have students read it, and ask what must happen to make it a long o word. Write the new word, *coat*, next to the original short vowel word. Have students read and change the remaining words on the board to *fine, pain/pane, seat,* and *tube*. Then, distribute a copy of the **Add a Vowel reproducible (page 82)** to pairs of students. Invite pairs to add the appropriate vowels to the words to make them long vowel words.

Extension: Make a set of flash cards that matches the number of students in the classroom. On each flash card, write either a short vowel word or its matching long vowel word. Distribute the flash cards randomly and let students find their matching pairs. If you have an odd number of students, use a short vowel word, *(such as pal)* that has two matching long vowel words *(pail and pale)*.

Which Word Doesn't Belong?

* CHALLENGE STUDENTS TO IDENTIFY SMALL WORDS IN LARGER WORDS TO IMPROVE DECODING SKILLS.

 **Directions** ➤

Practice the **Little Words in Big activity (page 60)** before doing this activity. Two of the words in each row have little words in them that you can see *and* hear. The third word (in bold type) does not. On the board, write one set of three words from the word list below.

Using blue pencils to draw boxes around the little words will help students' brains call more attention to them.

Word List:

1. small	forgive	**they**
2. rust	**one**	monkey
3. cabbage	pillow	**cover**
4. **great**	play	smile
5. **what**	dragon	folder
6. **find**	peach	scat
7. late	**time**	explain
8. puppet	mushroom	**hope**
9. absent	**bear**	skill
10. **early**	needle	hiccup
11. never	teacher	**heard**
12. saddle	**once**	boil
13. **paste**	return	slap
14. monster	think	**country**
15. microphone	**drown**	twig

Ask students to look at the three words on the board and determine which one doesn't belong because it does not have a little word inside that can be seen and heard. As students discuss the words, mark a blue box around the little words. The word that does not have a little word in it may look like it does. However, when you say the big word, you do not hear the little word. For example, you do not hear *eat* when you say the word *great*. Help students understand that they should draw boxes around only little words that they can see *and* hear. Ask students why they did not select all of the words. Discuss reasons why they may not hear the little word. For example, they do not hear the word *car* in the word *care* because the silent *e* makes the *a* say its name. Repeat this activity using two or three sets of words at a time.

Picture the Sound

* INTRODUCE NEW VOWEL COMBINATION SPELLINGS AND THE SOUNDS THAT GO WITH THEM.

 **Directions**

After students have worked extensively with short and long vowels, give each student a copy of the **Vowel Combination Picture Prompts cards (page 84)** to cut out. Review the sounds using the examples below. (Store the cards for further use.)

Remind students that once information enters the brain, it can be quickly dropped. Pictures grab the brain's attention. Information that is received visually using pictures is more easily retained and moves into the working memory. Adding a picture to a sound acts as a visual prompt to promote memory.

/oo/ (as in *foot*) = What the muscle man says when he picks up something heavy.
/oi/ /oy/ (as in *ahoy*) = What you yell when you see a ship.
/ou/ /ow/ (as in *mouse*) = What you say when you hit your thumb with a hammer.
/ar/ (as in *large*) = What a pirate says.
/au / /aw/ (as in *claw*) = What the boy says when he breaks his bat.
/oo/ (as in *boo*) = What the ghost says.

Explain that most of these vowel sounds are neither long nor short, but all are made with vowel combinations. Say each sound and have students repeat it and hold up the picture that goes with that sound. (Note that the /oo/ sound is often considered a long *u* sound. Adjust the cards and activity according to the teaching method your phonics program uses for this sound and vowel combination.)

Lightning Flash

* GIVE STUDENTS MORE PRACTICE IN IDENTIFYING VOWEL COMBINATION SOUNDS.

 **Directions**

Continue training students to see a two-letter pattern as one sound. Before the activity, use **index cards** to prepare flash cards of words from the **Vowel Combination Word List (page 85)**. Write consonants in black and vowel combinations spellings in color. Flip through the flash cards and ask students to look at the vowel pattern and say the vowel sounds. Increase the speed each time you flip through the cards until students' recognition of the vowel combinations becomes automatic.

Using color-coding will direct students' brains to pay attention to the vowel combinations in words.

Vowel Combination Response Cards

* HAVE STUDENTS PRACTICE IDENTIFYING VOWEL COMBINATION SOUNDS.

Again, using pictures will help students remember the sounds.

Directions ➤ Review the **Vowel Combination Picture Prompts (page 84)**. Give each student a set of cards to line up in a row. Say each vowel combination sound. Invite students to repeat the sound and hold up the appropriate card. Next, say words instead of just sounds. Tell students to listen to each word, repeat it aloud, and then hold up the vowel combination sound card they hear. Initially, use words from the **Vowel Combination Word List (page 85)** that begin with a vowel digraph (such as *out* and *oops*), and then move on to words in which the vowel digraph is in the middle. If students have trouble hearing the medial sound, remind them to use "hiccups" to emphasize the sound. Have them say the beginning of the word and then exaggerate the vowel combination by saying it three times before finishing the word. For example, say the word *pause*, then repeat it in exaggerated form, *p ... au...au...au...ause*.

Remind students that it is important for them to repeat each word after you. Explain that when you say the word, the students hear the word *outside* their heads. When they repeat the word themselves, they hear the word *inside* their heads. This makes it easier for them to hear and identify the sound.

~~~~~~

Find and List

* CONTINUE HAVING STUDENTS IDENTIFY VOWEL COMBINATION SPELLINGS AND WORDS.

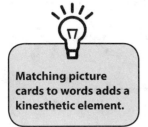

Matching picture cards to words adds a kinesthetic element.

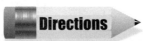

Directions ➤ Scan a **preselected story** for words with vowel digraphs. Cut apart and tape the **Vowel Combination Picture Prompts (page 84)** to the board. Leave space for words to be written below each card. After introducing the story, have students read it silently. Then ask students to reread and look for vowel digraph words. When a student finds a word with a vowel digraph, ask him or her to come to the board and write it under the appropriate picture. After students finish reading, have them read aloud the lists of words they wrote on the board. Discuss any words that were placed inaccurately and rewrite them under the appropriate pictures.

Short Vowel Picture Prompts

ă

ĕ

ĭ

ŏ

ŭ

Strategies For Struggling Readers © 2007 Creative Teaching Press

Short Vowel Word List
One-Syllable Words

Short A	Short E	Short I	Short O	Short U
act	bed	bid	box	bud
and	bet	big	cob	bug
ant	Ed	bit	cot	bun
at	elf	did	dot	bus
bad	end	dig	fog	but
bag	etch	dip	fox	cub
bat	fed	fin	got	cup
cab	hen	fit	hog	cut
can	jet	hid	hop	dug
cap	led	him	hot	fun
dad	leg	hip	job	gum
fan	let	hit	jot	hug
gas	men	if	log	hut
had	met	in	lot	mud
ham	net	inch	mom	nut
hat	pen	it	mop	pup
jam	red	itch	not	rub
lap	set	kid	odd	rug
mad	ten	kit	off	run
man	vet	lid	ox	sub
nap	web	lit	pond	sum
pal	wet	pig	pop	sun
ram	yes	pin	sob	tub
ran	yet	rib	top	tug
rap		rip		up
sad		sit		us
sat		six		
tag		tip		
tan		wig		
van		win		
wag		zip		

Short Vowel Word List
Consonant Blends and Digraphs

Short A	Short E	Short I	Short O	Short U
back	belt	blimp	blob	blunt
bath	bench	brick	block	brush
black	bled	chin	blot	buck
blast	blend	click	chop	bump
brag	bless	crib	clock	bunch
branch	check	dish	crop	bunt
brass	chest	drip	dock	club
catch	crest	flick	flock	clump
chat	deck	flip	flop	clunk
clam	desk	gift	frog	clutch
clamp	dress	itch	knock	crust
clash	fled	kick	knot	drug
crack	kept	lick	lock	drum
crash	left	pill	long	dunk
dash	mesh	shift	notch	fluff
drag	neck	ship	plod	grub
flag	nest	skin	plot	gruff
flash	peck	skip	pond	gust
glad	pest	slick	prop	lump
graph	press	slid	rock	mush
hatch	rest	sprint	shock	pluck
latch	shed	stick	shop	plug
match	shelf	swim	shot	pump
plant	sled	thick	slob	shrub
rash	slept	tick	slop	skunk
scratch	smell	trick	slot	slug
snap	spell	trim	sock	slump
splash	spent	trip	spot	snub
stamp	stem	twig	stock	struck
strand	step	whip	stop	strum
track	tent	wick	strong	stump
trap	wreck	wish	trot	trunk

Vowel-O Game Board

a e i o u

Word Line Word List

Short A

Ending Sound Manipulation

bad	bam	bat
cat	can	cab
gab	gap	gas
hat	ham	had
map	man	mad

Beginning Sound Manipulation

ham	bam	jam
cab	dab	nab
rack	sack	tack
sad	bad	dad
rag	bag	sag

Short E

Ending Sound Manipulation

bet	bed	beg
jet	Jeff	Jen
met	men	mess
leg	less	let
pet	pen	peg

Beginning Sound Manipulation

bed	fed	red
bet	wet	vet
pen	ten	yen
leg	beg	peg
led	wed	Ted

Short I

Ending Sound Manipulation

bib	bit	big
dig	did	dip
him	his	hit
lid	lip	lit
pig	pin	pit

Beginning Sound Manipulation

him	dim	rim
did	bid	hid
big	rig	dig
sit	fit	bit
hip	lip	dip

Short O

Ending Sound Manipulation

cob	cot	cop
dot	dog	doll
hop	hot	hog
job	jog	jot
lot	log	lox

Beginning Sound Manipulation

cob	Bob	job
pop	cop	hop
lot	pot	rot
cod	nod	pod
not	cot	dot

Short U

Ending Sound Manipulation

bud	bug	bun
cub	cut	cup
dug	dud	dull
gum	gull	gut
hug	hut	hum

Beginning Sound Manipulation

bud	mud	dud
sun	run	bun
bum	rum	sum
bug	hug	mug
nut	cut	hut

Strategies For Struggling Readers © 2007 Creative Teaching Press

Short Vowel Sound Puzzle

Name:_____

Making and Writing Words

Directions: Use the letters in the top boxes to make new words. Write your new words in the lower boxes.

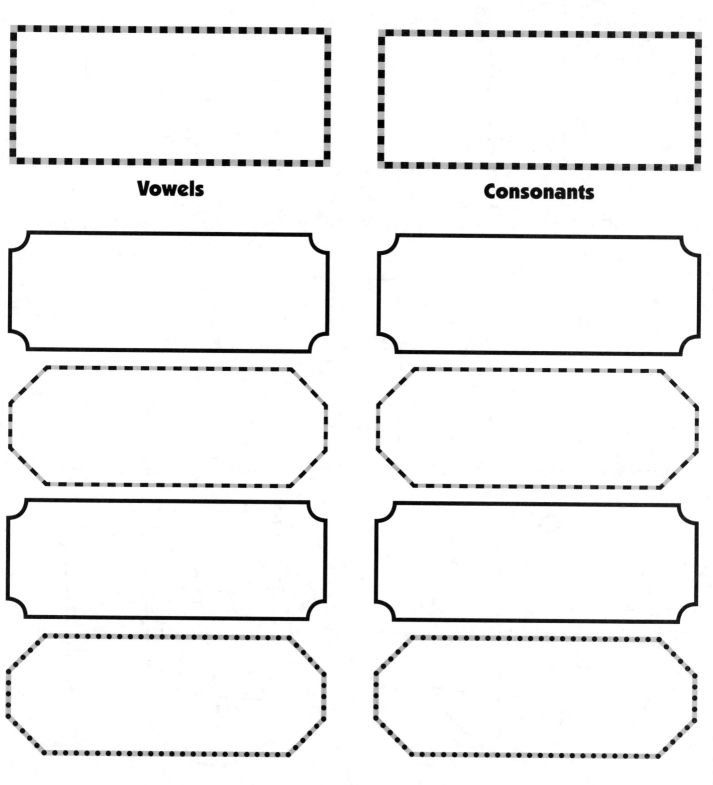

Vowels

Consonants

Strategies For Struggling Readers © 2007 Creative Teaching Press

Name:_____

Word Swap

Directions:

1. Change the beginning sound of the key word to make three new words. Write the new words in the "Beginning" column.
2. Change the middle sound of the key word to make three new words. Write the new words in the "Middle" column.
3. Change the ending sound of the key word to make three new words. Write the new words in the "Ending" column.

Key Word:

Beginning	Middle	Ending

  Bonus Words

Directions: Use the last word in each of the three sections above to make new words. This time, change two letters to make each new word, and write the words below.

Change last two letters.   Change first two letters.   Change first and last letters.

Strategies For Struggling Readers © 2007 Creative Teaching Press

Word Hunt

Directions: Draw a blue box around any little word you find in one of the big words. Remember, you have to be able to hear the little word when you say the big word. Read the little word and then the bigger word as you draw each blue box.

absent	factory	pillow
another	flour	planet
army	folder	play
astonish	forgive	pretend
attention	freezer	princess
bandage	giant	puppet
boil	hamster	reach
bonfire	harmful	recent
borrow	hiccup	repeat
bracelet	juggle	return
bring	late	rust
cabbage	layer	saddle
cancel	letter	scar
candle	litter	scat
carton	magnet	scrap
cattle	manage	season
clean	message	skill
cobweb	microphone	slap
cottage	monkey	small
customer	monster	smile
deliver	mushroom	spent
deserve	napkin	spring
dragon	needle	teacher
draw	never	team
electricity	newt	think
escape	passage	transparent
excuse	peach	twig
explain	peppermint	visit

Strategies For Struggling Readers © 2007 Creative Teaching Press

Word Hunt
Answer Key

absent (sent)
another (an, other)
army (arm)
astonish (on)
attention (ten)
bandage
  (an, and, ban, band)
boil (oil)
bonfire (on, fire)
borrow (row)
bracelet (brace, race, let)
bring (ring)
cabbage (cab)
cancel (can, an)
candle (can, and)
carton (car, art, ton)
cattle (cat, at)
clean (lean)
cobweb (cob, web)
cottage (cot)
customer (us, custom)
deliver (live, liver)
deserve (serve)
dragon (drag, rag, on)
draw (raw)
electricity (elect, city)
escape (cape, ape)
excuse (use)
explain (plain)

factory (fact, or, act)
flour (our)
folder (fold, old, older)
forgive (for, give)
freezer (free, freeze)
giant (ant)
hamster (am, ham, hams)
harmful (harm, arm)
hiccup (cup, up)
juggle (jug)
late (ate)
layer (lay)
letter (let)
litter (lit, it)
magnet (net)
manage (man, an)
message (mess)
microphone (phone)
monkey (monk, key)
monster (on)
mushroom (mush, room)
napkin (nap, kin)
needle (need)
never (ever)
newt (new)
passage (pass)
peach (pea, each)
peppermint
  (pepper, mint)

pillow (pill, low)
planet (plan, net)
play (lay)
pretend (ten, tend, end)
princess (prince)
puppet (pup, up, pet)
reach (each)
recent (cent)
repeat (eat)
return (turn)
rust (us)
saddle (ad, sad, add)
scar (car)
scat (cat, at)
scrap (rap)
season (sea, son)
skill (kill, ill)
slap (lap)
small (mall, all)
smile (mile)
spent (pen)
spring (ring)
teacher (tea, each)
team (tea)
think (ink)
transparent (ran, rent,
  an, spare, parent)
twig (wig)
visit (is, it)

Long Vowel Word List

Long A	Long E	Long I	Long O	Long U
a__e **(signal e)**	**e__e** **(signal e)**	**i__e** **(signal e)**	**o__e** **(signal e)**	**u__e** **(signal e)**
brave	Pete	drive	globe	cube
cake	here	hike	hope	cute
date	Steve	nine	robe	fuse
fade	these	shine	stove	huge
flame		side	those	mule
grape	**__ea__**	twine	woke	
shade	beach	wise		
whale	cheap			**__ew**
	each		**__oa__**	few
__ai__	leash	**__igh**	boat	knew
chain	scream	knight	goat	new
frail		right	soak	pew
main	**__ee__**	sigh	toad	stew
paint	cheek	tight	toast	
train	meet			
waist	sheep	**__y**	**__ow**	
wait	street	fly	bow	
	sweep	shy	flow	
__ay		sky	grow	
clay	**__y**	why	know	
hay	happy			
play	only			
stay	party			
tray	shiny			

Name:_____

What Makes Long Vowels Long?

Directions: Make tally marks in the appropriate boxes to indicate whether each word has a signal *e* or a "2-fer" spelling. Write the words on lines next to the tally boxes.

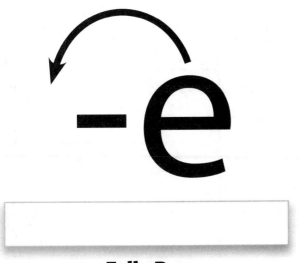

Tally Box

_____

_____

_____

_____

_____

Tally Box

_____

_____

_____

_____

Word Cards

Name:_____

Long Vowel Classification

Day #1

Day #2

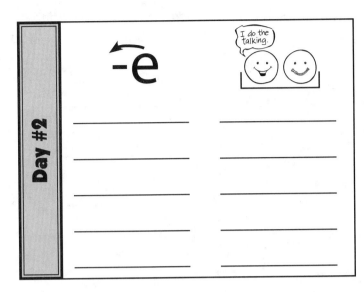

Day #3

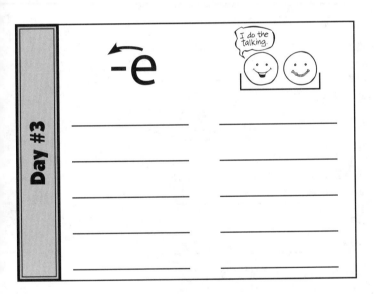

Day #4

Day #5

Add a Vowel

Directions: Read each short vowel word. Add the appropriate vowel to each word to change the short vowel into a long vowel. The first one is done for you.

1.	ad	_aid_	**33.**	lop	_____
2	at	_____	**34.**	mad	_____
3.	am	_____	**35.**	man	_____
4.	bat	_____	**36.**	mat	_____
5.	bed	_____	**37.**	men	_____
6.	Ben	_____	**38.**	met	_____
7.	bet	_____	**39.**	mop	_____
8.	bit	_____	**40.**	net	_____
9.	bled	_____	**41.**	not	_____
10.	blot	_____	**42.**	pad	_____
11.	brad	_____	**43.**	pal	_____
12.	bran	_____	**44.**	past	_____
13.	can	_____	**45.**	pep	_____
14.	cap	_____	**46.**	pet	_____
15.	clam	_____	**47.**	pin	_____
16.	con	_____	**48.**	plan	_____
17.	cub	_____	**49.**	plum	_____
18.	cut	_____	**50.**	quit	_____
19.	did	_____	**51.**	ran	_____
20.	din	_____	**52.**	rat	_____
21.	fad	_____	**53.**	red	_____
22.	fat	_____	**54.**	rid	_____
23.	fed	_____	**55.**	rip	_____
24.	gap	_____	**56.**	rod	_____
25.	got	_____	**57.**	rot	_____
26.	hat	_____	**58.**	run	_____
27.	hop	_____	**59.**	slat	_____
28.	hug	_____	**60.**	slid	_____
29.	kit	_____	**61.**	slop	_____
30.	lad	_____	**62.**	sop	_____
31.	led	_____	**63.**	spin	_____
32.	lest	_____	**64.**	spit	_____

Add a Vowel
Answer Key

1.	ad	ade, aid		**33.**	lop	lope
2.	at	ate		**34.**	mad	maid, made
3.	am	aim		**35.**	man	main, mane
4.	bat	bait, beat, boat		**36.**	mat	mate
5.	bed	bead		**37.**	men	mean
6.	Ben	bean		**38.**	met	meat, meet
7.	bet	beat, beet		**39.**	mop	mope
8.	bit	bite		**40.**	net	neat
9.	bled	bleed		**41.**	not	note
10.	blot	bloat		**42.**	pad	paid
11.	brad	braid		**43.**	pal	pale, pail
12.	bran	brain		**44.**	past	paste
13.	can	cane		**45.**	pep	peep
14.	cap	cape		**46.**	pet	Pete
15.	clam	claim		**47.**	pin	pine
16.	con	cone		**48.**	plan	plane, plain
17.	cub	cube		**49.**	plum	plume
18.	cut	cute		**50.**	quit	quite
19.	did	died		**51.**	ran	rain
20.	din	dine		**52.**	rat	rate
21.	fad	fade		**53.**	red	read
22.	fat	fate		**54.**	rid	ride
23.	fed	feed		**55.**	rip	ripe
24.	gap	gape		**56.**	rod	road
25.	got	goat		**57.**	rot	rote
26.	hat	hate		**58.**	run	ruin
27.	hop	hope		**59.**	slat	slate
28.	hug	huge		**60.**	slid	slide
29.	kit	kite		**61.**	slop	slope
30.	lad	laid, lady		**62.**	sop	soap
31.	led	lead		**63.**	spin	spine
32.	lest	least		**64.**	spit	spite

Vowel Combination Picture Prompts

oo

oi__   __oy

ou__   __ow

ar

au__   __aw

oo

Vowel Combination Word List

/oo/ as in school

brood	oops	root	spool
goof	pool	shoot	tool
mood			

/oo/ as in good

foot	look	stood
good	shook	wood

/oi/ and /oy/ as in toy

boil	coin	joy	soil
boy	join	oil	toy

/ar/ as in car

ark	bark	chart	shark
arm	cart	large	star
art	charge	scar	yard

/ow/ and /ou/ as in hour

bounce	loud	out	south
cloud	mouth	pound	
couch	ouch	sound	

/au/ and /aw/ as in awful

autumn	crawl	haunt	paw
awful	flaunt	launch	
caught	flaw	lawn	

Vocabulary and Word Recognition

Readers need to know the meanings of words in order to understand text. Students learn most of their vocabulary indirectly—by hearing words repeated in different contexts—but direct instruction is still important because students need to develop word-learning strategies that include using context, visualizing, and using word associations and reference skills. All of these strategies help students activate prior knowledge, build word relationships, and connect with the text. Wide reading is another significant contributor to vocabulary development. However, students who need the most reading practice generally spend the least amount of time actually reading. Giving students sufficient time to read will help increase their exposure to and practice with words.

Prerequisite Skills in Vocabulary

In order to construct meaning from text, struggling readers need to do the following:

- Demonstrate word awareness: the desire to know words and gain satisfaction from making them part of spoken and written vocabulary.

- Use alternative (unknown) words to construct meaning.

- Be able to attach a new concept to an existing one (prior knowledge).

- Use the context surrounding an unknown word to discover its meaning.

- Be cognitively aware of using words to form relationships and connections.

- Link verbal and visual images to store new vocabulary in long-term memory.

Recommendations

To develop a rich vocabulary, students need literacy experiences that integrate listening, speaking, reading, and writing. Direct instruction usually involves discussion prior to reading. This instruction should involve CPR—using context, activating prior knowledge, and reinforcing new words in many meaningful ways. Generally, only five to seven vocabulary words should be highlighted for a specific story. These should be words that are central to understanding the topic, and they should be difficult but useful words that the students will meet again in text.

Spider Map

* HELP STUDENTS MAKE PERSONAL CONNECTIONS TO NEW VOCABULARY.

Using graphic organizers is similar to using pictures.

 **Directions**

Select a word from students' guided reading or another current vocabulary list. This word should be easy to define and describe. Distribute the **Spider Map reproducible (page 97)** to each student. Explain that the brain remembers new information better when it is connected to prior knowledge—something they already know. The Spider Map will help students make connections to the new word and develop personal meanings for it. Direct students to write the new word on the spider's head, a one- or two-word definition on the body, four descriptive words on the right legs, and four examples of the word on the left legs. Collaboratively complete a Spider Map for the pre-selected vocabulary word before students complete one on their own.

Extension: When reading a new story as a class, let each student choose a significant story word and complete a spider map for it. Tell students not to write the words on the spiders' heads. Have students trade papers and see if they can guess each other's words.

Connect Four

* GIVE STUDENTS PRACTICE IN APPLYING NEW VOCABULARY IN CONTEXT.

Students will use the same word several times in different ways to get needed practice. Use this activity within 18–24 hours after introducing a new word to concur with brain-based learning instruction.

 **Directions**

Preselect **vocabulary words** from students' reading material. Tackle one word at a time. Using the following formats, invite students to write four sentences using a new vocabulary word. In sentence #1, students should use the word appropriately in context. In sentence #2, students should describe the characteristics or attributes of the word. In sentence #3, students should write a definition for the vocabulary word. In sentence #4, students should relate the new word to their lives. For example, if using *aroma* as the preselected vocabulary word, a student may write *Pumpkin pie has a delicious* **aroma**, *An* **aroma** *can be pleasant or bad*, *An* **aroma** *is an odor*, and *The* **aroma** *of pumpkin pie reminds me of Thanksgiving.*

Relationship Box

Select **10 words** from assigned reading that are critical to understanding the text. List those words on the board along with the page numbers where they appear. Give each student a copy of the **Relationship Box reproducible (page 98)**. Ask each student to choose three or four words from the list, read each passage that contains a word he or she selected, then complete a three-section relationship box for each word. To complete a box, students should write a chosen word in the first section, draw a picture of the word's meaning in the second section, and write a synonym for the word in the last section. When students have finished, call on a volunteer to share a relationship box for each word on the list.

Allowing students to select their own words from a list lets them decide what is important. They will also create pictures to reinforce their learning.

Start and Stop

Preview a **text selection** and mark focus words that need extra attention. Teach students the start-and-stop reading technique. As you model reading the story, stop before reaching one of the preselected words and have students read that word.

Making a game out of reading will help students learn the emphasized words.

Extension: When students are reading independently, consider letting a student choose several focus words—words he or she finds difficult or important. Do a start-and-stop reading with the class using this student's words as the focus words.

Synonym Stairs

* HELP STUDENTS EXPAND THEIR REPERTOIRE OF WORD MEANINGS FOR CHOSEN WORDS.

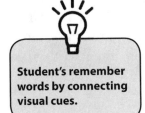

By identifying synonyms, the students are reinforcing meaning and applying it in different ways.

 **Directions** ➤ Make a **list of words** that are easily definable and have numerous synonyms. (Guided reading vocabulary often works well.) Write these words on the board. Divide students into teams. Give each team a vocabulary word and a copy of the **Synonym Stairs reproducible (page 99)**. Have each team brainstorm lists of synonyms for the word and write each word on a stair step. Have students share completed synonym stairs.

Extension: Make this activity kinesthetic. On a piece of sentence strip, write a word for which there are many synonyms. Conceal the word from students. Give

each student an index card and a marker, and then take the class to a flight of stairs. Reveal the word and let students write synonyms on their index cards. As each student finishes writing, have him or her choose a stair step to stand on and share the synonym with the class. If several students choose the same synonym, let them stand on consecutive steps, or one behind the other on the same step if there is room. Back in the classroom, post the original word and synonyms in a stair-step pattern on a bulletin board.

Frame It

* TEACH STUDENTS TO VISUALIZE WORDS IN DIFFERENT WAYS.

Student's remember words by connecting visual cues.

 **Directions** ➤ Write a list of **vocabulary words** on the board. Give each student **markers** or **crayons**. Invite each student or pair of students to select one word from the list. Distribute a copy of the **Word Frame reproducible (page 100)** to each student or pair and model how to complete the page.

1. In the large box in the middle of the page, draw a picture of the selected word.
2. In the top right section, write the word.
3. In the top left section, write a short definition of the word.
4. In the bottom left section, write a synonym for the word.
5. In the bottom right section, write an antonym for the word.

Let students use colored markers or crayons to write their words, draw pictures, and decorate the frames. After students have completed their frames, have them share them with the rest of the class. Display the frames in the classroom.

Classify It

* TEACH STUDENTS TO UNDERSTAND WORD FUNCTIONS AND RELATIONSHIPS.

Having students write words within the same category in the same colors reinforces their learning and the connections between the words.

Directions

Write a **list of related words** on the board. Draw a few columns next to the list. At the top of each column, draw a question mark. Begin by having students read aloud the list of words. Explain that they should decide on categories and then sort the words into the categories. Students may choose categories related to word meanings, words with similar structure (such as words that end in -*ed*), words with double letters, or big words that have little words in them. (See example.)

Description of a Thing	Emotions	Words with Double Letters
wrinkled	furious	deep
deep	worried	worried
flat	relieved	

Assign students to groups, provide markers and chart paper, and have groups begin listing the categories on the chart paper and assigning words to them. (Students should write each separate category and list in a different color.) When the categorizing is complete, have one group's volunteer read one set of grouped words without stating the category. Have other teams guess what category the group chose. Allow other groups to share different word groupings.

Criss-Cross Sentences

* GIVE STUDENTS MORE PRACTICE WITH USING CONTEXT CLUES TO FIND WORD MEANINGS.

When students build a relationship between words it helps them remember the meaning.

Directions

After reading a story as a class, make **two lists of words**. In the first list, write story words that were difficult for students. In the second list, in random order, write related words or synonyms for words in the first list.

List 1	List 2
furious	upset
worried	looked
glanced	angry

Ask students to read the two lists and discuss words that might go together. Have students write sentences using the words. Each sentence must contain a word from the first column and its matching word from the second column. Invite volunteers to read their sentences.

See It, Say It

* TRAIN STUDENTS TO COMBINE PHONETIC OR GRAPHIC CLUES WITH PRIOR KNOWLEDGE TO DISCOVER WORD MEANINGS.

Word recognition is strengthened by recognizing letter order and patterns.

 **Directions** ➤ This activity is a spin-off of the hangman game. Select **six story words** that were interesting or important to the meaning of a recent reading assignment. After students have completed the reading, have them number sheets of paper from one to six as you do the same on the board. Next to the number one, draw blanks for each letter in the first word from your list. Have students do the same thing on their papers. Tell students that they will be trying to guess the story word by looking at the letters and thinking about what happened in the story. Write the first letter on the first blank, pause, and then write the second letter. Keep adding letters until the word is correctly identified. Discuss what strategies students used to determine the word. Have students write that word in the appropriate blank on their papers. Continue with the remaining words.

Use It or Lose It

* EXPAND STUDENTS' VOCABULARIES AND GIVE THEM OPPORTUNITIES TO USE NEW WORDS IN CONTEXT.

Using the word in different contexts builds word recogniton and word meaning.

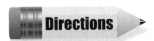 **Directions** ➤ After discussing new **vocabulary words** from a story, choose three or four of the most challenging words. Discuss the meanings of the words and write them on the board. Explain that using new words in conversation will help students remember them. Challenge students to correctly use each vocabulary word three different times throughout the day. Make a game of it by keeping a tally of the number of times each word is used.

What's Missing?

* DEMONSTRATE USING CONTEXT CLUES TO IDENTIFY UNFAMILIAR (OR MISSING) WORDS.

Monitoring reading to see what makes sense increases comprehension.

 **Directions** ▶ Write a simple passage that relates to a story topic. Replace some of the key words with blanks and make a transparency of the story passage. Or make an **overhead transparency** of the passage below.

Long _____, the Emperor welcomed _____ Mulan to the High Palace. First, a soldier _____ a huge drum. Then the Emperor _____ a speech about how _____ gave up everything and _____ the army. He won _____ because he was so _____ and skilled. Now the _____ is safe from the _____.

Introduce the concept of using context clues to determine the meaning of an unfamiliar word. Read the transparency passage aloud as a class, skipping the blanks. As students read each sentence, pause to ask comprehension questions about its meaning. When students finish reading the passage, ask how they were able to understand the overall meaning of the passage and answer the questions, even though some of the key words are missing. If students have trouble putting the concept into words, explain that sometimes they can use what they know from the surrounding words to understand what the missing words could be.

Poppers

* TEACH STUDENTS TO COMBINE AUDITORY AND CONTEXT CLUES TO IDENTIFY UNFAMILIAR WORDS.

Introduce the Strategy #6 icon on the Strategies Bookmark (page 8), and have students refer to it in order to help them remember to apply the strategy. The picture will help them remember the strategy during their own reading.

 **Directions** ▶ Preview a **text selection**. Prepare it by deleting key words, leaving only the beginning letter for each word. Read the passage to students. When you come to a deleted word, say the beginning sound and stop. For example, read, *Hearing the ring, he quickly answered the ph_____.* Students will readily supply the correct word. Ask how they knew the word if they couldn't see it. Tell students that sometimes, if they just say the beginning sound of the unknown word, the word might just "pop" out. Continue reading the sentences aloud with students, helping them use "poppers" to identify the missing words.

Give It Meaning

* DEMONSTRATE HOW TO USE SENTENCE CONTEXT CLUES TO UNDERSTAND MEANING.

Students use the rest of the sentence to determine the meaning of unknown words.

 **Directions** ➤ Copy or write a **paragraph** that describes a story plot that students are reading, or use the sample: *Mona lost her hat again. She looked in the* **Lunt** *and Found box. She only saw lost jackets and* **thists**. *She kept* **biming** *for it but could not find it. Finally, at the bottom of the* **jix** *she found her* **hon**. Write each sentence on a separate **sentence strip**. Place the sentence strips, in order, in a **pocket chart**. Next, write a few nonsense words on **index cards**. Place each nonsense words over a key word in the paragraph.

Explain that being able to pronounce words may not always help students understand what the words mean. But, even though they may not know all of the words, they can still figure out the meaning of the text. As a class, read the paragraph in the pocket chart. When you come to a nonsense word, pause and ask students what that word should be. Discuss what students must do to figure out what the word should be. Encourage students to keep reading the entire sentence as they look for clues to help them know the word's meaning. Continue reading until the story is completed.

Extension: Repeat this activity 18–24 hours later with a different text. Let students write the nonsense words on index cards and use their cards for this activity.

~~~~~~

The Missing Link

* USE CLUES TO DETERMINE THE MEANING OF UNKNOWN ADJECTIVES AND ADVERBS.

Refer students to Strategy #2 in the Strategies Bookmark (page 8). Help students use the icon to help them recall this strategy.

 **Directions** ➤ Write several **sentences** that contain context clues on the board, such as: *The* gigantic *bear was as* large *as a house.* In each sentence, underline a key word that is defined in the next part of the sentence. Have students read the first sentence. Explain that sentences often contain clue words or "missing links" that can help them define unfamiliar words. Point to the underlined word and ask students to find the clue word in the sentence that helps them understand the word's meaning. Underline the clue word, and draw a line to link the two words together. Discuss the importance of using context clues to determine the meaning of unknown words. Invite students to underline and connect the word pairs in the rest of the sentences you have prepared.

Scavenger Hunt

*TEACH STUDENTS HOW TO USE WORD STRUCTURE CLUES TO DECODE WORDS.

Seeing "chunks" and word patterns inside a word increases word recognition and speeds up decoding.

Also, refer to Strategy #4 from the Strategies Bookmark (page 8).

 **Directions** ➤ On the board, write a list of **nonsense words** that contain real smaller words within them, such as *sment, frun, finst,* and *zand*. Ask students to read the nonsense words. Explain that they are not real words. As students begin to read the words, ask if there are any clues to the nonsense words. If students hesitate, point to one of the words and ask them if they see anything familiar. Explain that sometimes, there might be a little word inside a bigger word. Draw a box around each little word inside a nonsense word. Ask students if it is now easier for them to read the words. Have them read the words together, saying the little word first and then the bigger word.

Give each student a copy of the **Scavenger Hunt reproducible (page 101)**. Explain that some of the words are nonsense words and a few are real words. Ask students to go on a little word scavenger hunt and draw a box around each little word they find inside a bigger word. When they are finished, have students read the list of words, saying the little word and then the big word.

Extension: Create a set of classroom labels from index cards. Include some nonsense words among the real words. Make sure that in each big word, a little word can be found. Attach the labels to their objects and have students go on a scavenger hunt to bring you all of the nonsense words. Collect all of the real words, post them in a pocket chart, and have students take turns circling the little words in the big words. Possible real words to use as labels include *chalkboard (chalk, board), door (or), window (win, wind), teacher (each), bulletin board (bull, tin, oar), floor (or), notebook (note, book), textbook (text, book), hallway (hall, way), globe (lobe),* and *pencil (pen).*

Guess My Word

* HELP STUDENTS USE LETTER PATTERNS IN VOCABULARY WORDS TO REINFORCE WORD RECOGNITION.

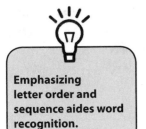

Emphasizing letter order and sequence aides word recognition.

 **Directions** ➤ Choose **vocabulary words** from a recent story. Write each word on a separate **index card**. Fold the cards in half and place them in a **paper bag**. Ask a student to select a card from the bag and give it to you without looking at it. Write the middle letter of the word on the board and add blanks on either side for the remaining letters. Return the word card to the student who selected it. Ask the remaining students to guess the word. Have the student with the word card add another letter to the left or right of the middle letter that was already written on the board. With each incorrect guess, the student should add another letter, moving outward from the center. The first student to guess the word and give the meaning gets to choose the next word card.

Letter Snatcher

* TEACH STUDENTS TO COMBINE PRIOR KNOWLEDGE, LETTER PATTERNS, AND CONTEXT CLUES TO IDENTIFY WORDS.

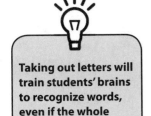

Taking out letters will train students' brains to recognize words, even if the whole word is not known.

 **Directions** ➤ On a **transparency**, write text from a student **reading selection**, or use the one below. Delete the vowels or beginning sounds. Make a copy of the following Letter Snatcher passage for each student.

Dr__gons have sk__n much __ike snak__s, li__ards, and other r__ptiles. Since they ar__ __old-blo__ded, d__agons l__ke to liv__ in __arm sp__ts.

Distribute the Letter Snatcher page to students. Explain that letters have been "snatched" from some of the words in the passage. Have students read the text as it appears. Tell students that the story context will help them fill in the gaps. Guide students to say the sounds, look at letter patterns, and search for context clues. Add the missing letters on the transparency as students add the letters on their papers. Read the completed passage and discuss how students were able to read the words.

Mystery Words

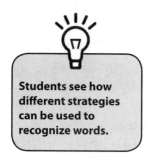

Students see how different strategies can be used to recognize words.

Directions ▸ Select **vocabulary words** from text. Make a list of clues to help students identify the words. The clues can refer to the meaning of the word, the phonetic structure, the letters, or a phonemic awareness characteristic (rhyming word or number of syllables). Some examples are:

Find a word that has the /ou/ sound.
Find a word that means *to do over and over*.
Find a word with double letters.
Find a word that rhymes with *station*.
Find a word that has both short /i/ and long/i/.

Invite students to open their books to the text selection. Give clues to help them find the mystery words in the story, and have students write the answers on sheets of paper. When students have found the words, have them read the passage aloud independently. Discuss the passage and the words afterward, asking students if they feel like they understand the passage better since they were introduced to parts of it before reading.

Extension: Pair students and assign a new passage to the class. Instruct the pairs to think of new clues for words that they think are important. Allow the pairs to swap sets of clues and find the answers within the story. Ask students which words they think they know better: the ones they found or the ones for which they wrote the clues.

Spider Map

Directions: Write a new word on the spider's head. Write a one- or two-word definition for that key word on the spider's body. Write a describing word for the key word on each of the right legs. Write an example of the key word on each of the left legs.

Relationship Box

Directions: Write a key word in the first box. Draw a picture of the key word's meaning in the second box. Write a synonym for the key word in the third box.

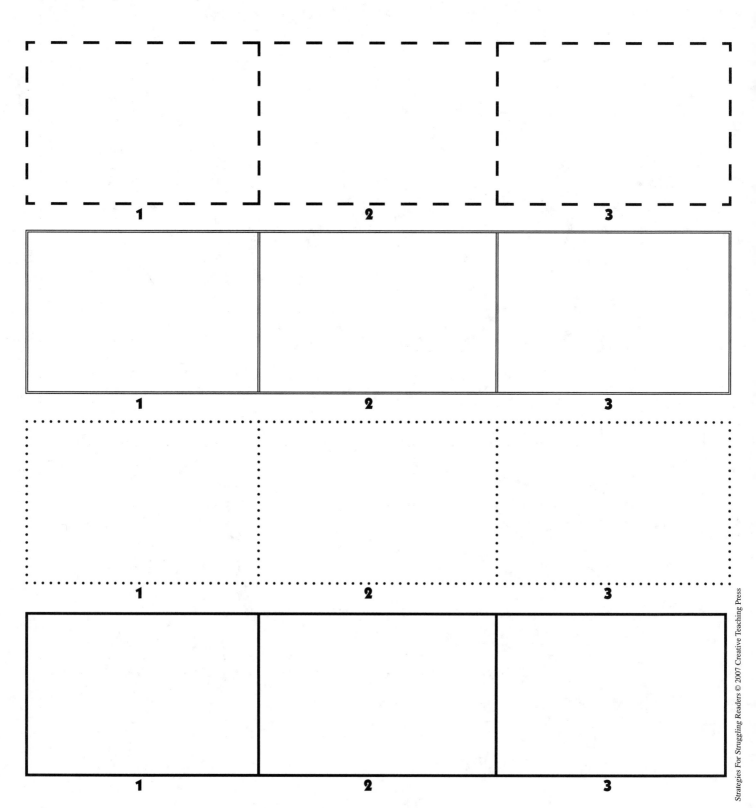

Name: _____

Synonym Stairs

Directions: Write a key word on the bottom step. Write a synonym (word that means the same) for the key word on each of the other steps.
How many steps can you climb?

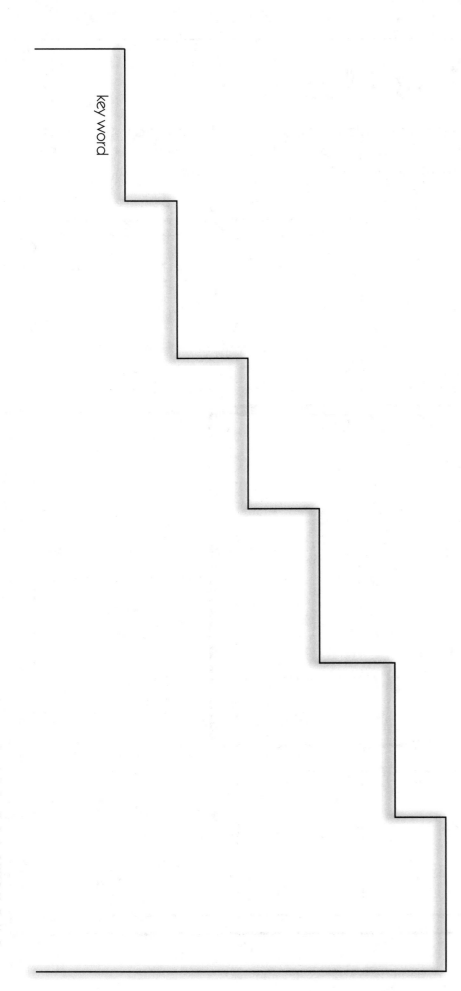

key word

Word Frame

Directions: Draw a picture of a key word in the middle of the frame. Write the key word in the top right section. Write a definition for the key word in the top left section. Write a synonym for the key word in the bottom left section. Write an antonym for the key word in the bottom right section.

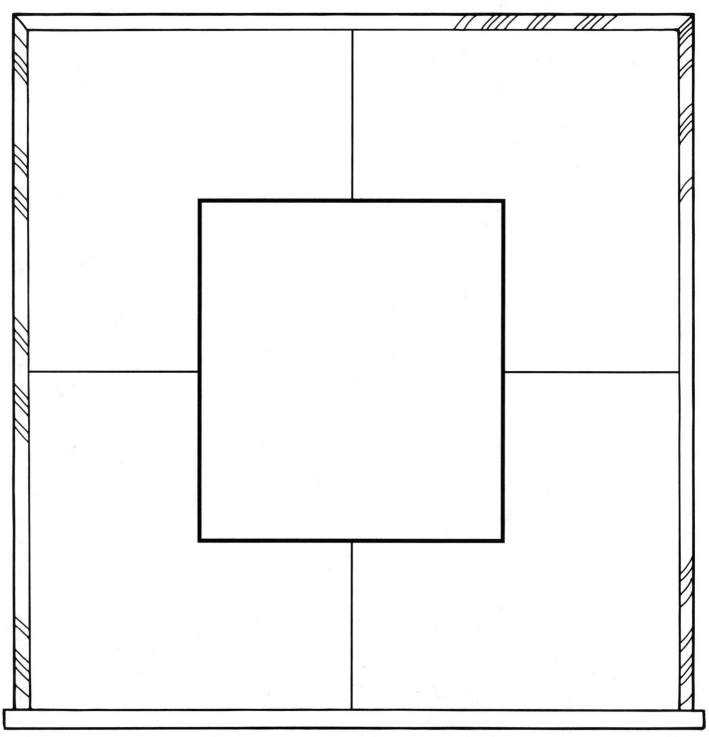

Scavenger Hunt

Directions: Draw a box around each little word you find inside a bigger word.

flill	ponud	grat
thin	stin	chorn
leat	mall	onstoo
busp	ballo	fit
thisk	smust	tent
sled	wins	zill
stwig	boxes	menz
clap	inth	slif
fast	pout	fint
thand	upset	jand
cold	larm	stop
plip	twin	ufog

Scavenger Hunt
Answer Key

flill (ill)

thin (in)

leat (eat)

busp (us, bus)

thisk (this, his, is)

sled (led)

stwig (twig, wig)

clap (lap)

fast (as)

thand (and, hand, than, an)

cold (old)

plip (lip)

ponud (on)

stin (tin, in)

mall (all)

ballo (ball, all)

smust (must, us)

wins (win, in)

boxes (ox, box)

inth (in)

pout (out)

upset (up, set)

larm (arm)

twin (win, in)

grat (rat, at)

chorn (or, horn)

onstoo (on, to, too)

fit (it)

tent (ten)

zill (ill)

menz (men)

slif (if)

fint (in, fin)

jand (and, an)

stop (top)

ufog (fog)

Fluency

Fluency bridges the gap between word recognition and comprehension. Children who lack fluency read aloud slowly and laboriously, making it difficult for them to remember what they read and to connect or relate to the text. Since most of their cognitive energy is directed toward print processing, little attention is left for comprehension. Having good fluency also means using skillful phrasing, intonation, pitch, and expression when reading aloud. Struggling readers look at each word independently rather than chunking words into phrases. Additionally, these readers are not automatic in word recognition and phrasing, which makes it impossible for them to read aloud with ease.

Students need specific fluency instruction and frequent reading practice with texts at their independent reading levels. Assisted and repeated oral readings of the same text provide systematic and explicit guidance and feedback to students. Independent, silent reading fosters both fluency and vocabulary development. Short, intense daily practice that extends over weeks and months, with students rereading passages until they attain high accuracy, can also develop fluency. The automatic word recognition skills gained with practice positively impacts comprehension.

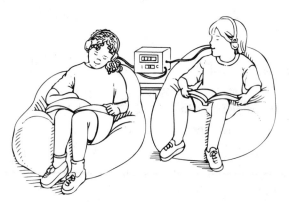

Prerequisite Skills in Fluency

In order to read fluently and with expression, struggling readers need to do the following:

- Understand and identify noun, verb, and prepositional phrases.

- "Chunk" text into grammatically meaningful phrases.

- Recognize that punctuation marks require a pause in reading.

- Convey text mood and meaning through appropriate expression and tone.

- Make a conversational connection in their reading.

- Recognize words automatically so that energy can be directed to comprehension.

Recommendations

Repeated readings of all kinds, especially of poetry, help students learn to read with expression, develop the skill of chunking text into meaningful phrases, and orally interpret the text. The rhythm and rhyme in poetry also help students make their reading sound more like conversation. Finally, using music with lyrics for fluency practice also supports brain-based learning.

Echo Reading

* ALLOW STUDENTS TO ECHO MODELED READING TO IMPROVE CADENCE AND EXPRESSION.

In this activity and its extension, students will combine visual and auditory learning.

Directions ▸ Choose a few sentences from a **text selection** to read aloud. Practice beforehand to ensure that you will read them fluently. Read the first sentence and model appropriate expression, intonation, and phrasing. Invite students to echo the reading, making it sound exactly like your reading. After modeling a few sentences, ask students what you did with your voice as you were reading. If necessary, prompt students with questions like *Did my voice go up or down in spots? Did I read faster in some places? Did I put more emphasis on some words? Did I sound happy, sad, excited, or scared?* Repeat with other sentences.

Extension: For visual reinforcement, write a sentence on the board and read it aloud. Have students tell you what you did with your voice as you read. Mark the sentence accordingly. Use colored chalk or marker to draw arrows to indicate voice inflection, underline words that you emphasized, draw lines to link words that you chunked together, and draw faces to show expression.

Collaborative Reading

* PREVIEW STORY VOCABULARY TO INCREASE FLUENCY.

Previewing and discussing illustrations before reading helps students attach meaning to words and make connections.

Directions ▸ Choose a new **text selection** that will be effective when combined with a picture walk. As you conduct the picture walk, discuss the pictures using challenging or new vocabulary words from the text. Next, read the story aloud. (If the story is long, divide it into segments.) Invite students to join in when they are comfortable. After the picture walk, have students reread silently. Group students who need more support and read the story with them.

Every Other Story

* HAVE STUDENTS FOCUS ON EXPRESSION AND PHRASING WHILE READING ALOUD.

Using color in this activity will capture students' attention, as will the novel approach of simply drawing lines rather than writing text.

Before the activity, choose a **text selection** that is at students' independent reading level and that is especially effective when read with good expression and phrasing. Introduce the selection by drawing colored lines that represent writing on the board. Make the first line one color and place a period at the end. Use a different color to make the second line and place a period at the end. Continue making alternating colored lines using the same two colors. Ask students to tell you something about these lines. Students should identify the two colors, recognize the periods, and identify the alternating color pattern. Explain that students will recognize this pattern in the activity.

Next, distribute **copies of the text selection** or write it on the board. Read the first sentence. When you stop, let students read the second sentence. Continue with students reading every other line. Note that students will attempt to match your reading rate. They will also be exposed to context clues in the sentences that you read, which will help them recognize words that appear in their sentences.

Speeding Ticket

* HAVE STUDENTS READ TEXT MULTIPLE TIMES TO IMPROVE FLUENCY.

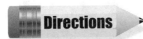

Creating the picture cards adds motivation for repeated reading. Flipping over the cards adds a kinesthetic element.

Text should be read one time to gain understanding (comprehension) and a second time for speed (fluency). Remind students that the more they practice, the better they will become at reading smoothly and with expression and speed. Give each student an **index card**. Have students write the word *speed* on their cards, making the letters look as if they are going fast. Have students **tape** these cards to the edges of their desks and then flip over the cards on their desktops to hide the word *speed*. Invite

students to read a **text selection** one time for comprehension. As students finish this first reading, have them flip down their cards to show the word *speed*, and then read the text a second time for fluency and speed.

Partner Reading

* HAVE STUDENTS READ TEXT MULTIPLE TIMES TO IMPROVE FLUENCY.

Completing multiple practice runs over two days fulfills the recommended 18 to 24 hour time span and allows students to see that practice is improving their reading.

 Designate a spot in the classroom for several **"partner reading" books**. To qualify for partner reading, books should be at students' independent reading levels. Explain that when students read a book more than once, they make fewer mistakes, increase their reading speed, and read with more expression. Designate one or two days per week for partner reading. Before the first partner reading day of each week, ask each student to choose a reading passage from a partner reading book and complete a practice reading. Then let students read their selections three times to three different partners. After each reading, have the listening partner complete the **Partner Reading Checklist (page 112)** to indicate how the reading partner did. After the third reading, have each student note progress by reviewing the checklists filled out by classmates.

Reading Workout

* CONTINUE HAVING STUDENTS READ THE TEXT MULTIPLE TIMES TO IMPROVE FLUENCY.

This activity helps students monitor their own reading and see how they can help themselves improve.

 In a quiet corner of the classroom, provide reading passages at students' independent reading levels along with cassette tapes and a tape recorder. Explain that when athletes want to build muscles and improve strength, they must exercise those muscles by repeatedly lifting weights. When runners want to improve their speed, they must run repeatedly and time themselves so that they can determine if their speed is improving. If readers want to get stronger and read faster, they have to work out to build their "reading muscles." Have students choose text selections and read them once for comprehension. Then have students tape-record their second readings of the passages. Invite students to listen to their readings and make notations on copies of the **Reading Workout Record (page 112)**. They should listen for whether they are recognizing words faster, using expression, or grouping words together. Invite students to record themselves again as they read a third time. During this reading, they should strive to improve in the areas highlighted in their notes. As students listen to the taped readings, invite them to review their Reading Workout Records to note improvements.

Reader's Theater

* HAVE STUDENTS READ A SCRIPT MULTIPLE TIMES TO IMPROVE FLUENCY.

 Develop a **Reader's Theater script** from a narrative text selection students are reading. To accommodate lower-level readers, substitute easier text and vocabulary as needed. Commercial Reader's Theater scripts are available, but using students' own reading material helps reinforce the vocabulary in and comprehension of text students will be reading independently. Distribute a **script** to each student. Read it together and discuss the characters, setting, and plot. Have students practice reading the script and then decide as a group who will play each part. Explain that there are a limited number of parts. Students who are not assigned a part will be audience members and will get first choice for parts in the next Reader's Theater activity. (If you want all students to read, create narrator roles that can be read by a group.) Give students additional practice time, and then have them perform the Reader's Theater for the audience.

> Using Reader's Theater will be novel to students. Working together to put on a performance creates a positive classroom environment that can improve students' attitudes.

Extension: Consider inviting parents or a younger class to the reading.

Go-Togethers

* HAVE STUDENTS FOCUS SPECIFICALLY ON PHRASING AND PACING.

 Copy some of the phrases from the **Go-Togethers reproducible (page 113)** on **sentence strips** and place them in a **pocket chart**. Show students the phrases and explain that phrases are words that go together. Have students read the first phrase aloud and then count the number of words. Tell students that these words go together and can be read together as one. Demonstrate by reading the words separately and then as a phrase (all in one breath), showing that reading in phrases will increase reading speed.

> Combining color with the curved lines adds a graphic element. Grouping words into phrases is a form of chunking—making a smaller workload for the brain's working memory desk.

Extension: Invite students to practice phrases from their reading material. Write each sentence on a sentence strip. Write the highlighted phrase in color and the rest of the text in black. Draw a curved line under the colored words to show that they are to be read together. Choose a sentence to read word by word, with a slight pause between each word. Reread the sentence and link appropriate words together. Ask students to compare the two readings and decide what was different. Explain that grouping words into phrases increases reading speed and makes the reading sound more like natural conversation.

Reading Aerobics

* HELP STUDENTS UNDERSTAND THE IMPORTANCE OF PUNCTUATION IN COMPREHENDING TEXT AND READING IT FLUENTLY.

> **Adding walking to reading adds a kinesthetic element. Working on the playground is something new and different.**

Directions ▶ Choose a passage from students' reading, copy it, and redistribute the punctuation. It should look something like this: *I'll never learn wailed. The teeny tiny ghost I'm so. Timid I scare myself and a teeny tiny tear. Slid down his cheek his teeny tiny cats. Climbed on his lap licked. His teeny tiny face purred their teeny tiny purrs.*

Begin the activity by reading the **text selection** with the new punctuation. Ask students if the passage made sense. Ask them why not, since it is a selection from their reading material. Help students understand that punctuation helps keep ideas together and makes it easier to read text correctly. Explain that the brain needs punctuation because text is usually printed in lines, and the sentences don't always end at the end of a line, so it is easy to misplace punctuation. Every time there is a pause or a stop, the brain gets a chance to think about what it has read (or *recode*) and can use that information to make sense of what will be read next. If the reader doesn't pause, or pauses at the wrong place, the brain cannot make sense of what was read.

Let students take their books to an open space, such as the playground. Have them form one long line facing the open space. Ask students to walk as they read aloud together. When they come to a period or question mark, they should stop. When they come to a comma, semicolon, or dash, they should pause by holding up one foot, waiting a second, and then taking their next step.

Laser Reading

* HELP STUDENTS UNDERSTAND HOW GROUPING WORDS INTO PHRASES INCREASES READING SPEED.

> **Continue chunking words into phrases and creating a smaller workload for the brain's working memory desk. Using the laser light adds something novel to the activity.**

Directions ▶ Remind students that reading words in phrases increases reading speed. Demonstrate how to read along with a laser light. Show a transparency of a text selection students are reading. As students read aloud, shine the light on the words, moving it along at a consistent, steady pace. After the reading, tell students to reread the passage. Move the light faster this time and encourage students to keep up with it. Congratulate students for pushing themselves to improve their pacing and reading speed.

Eye Counting

* TEACH STUDENTS TO USE SPECIFIC STRATEGIES TO REDUCE CHOPPY READING CADENCE.

Increasing the visual span contributes to increasing reading rate and fluency, resulting in back-brain reading.

Since many struggling readers have developed the habit of choppy, word-by-word reading, they need help learning how to see more words as they read. Explain that the eye's visual span is very important in reading. The eye's visual span determines how many symbols the eye can take in at one time. For beginning readers, the visual unit is letter by letter. As students read more, their visual span increases and the eye can take in whole words. When students read a passage for the first time, their visual unit is smaller. As they reread and the words become more familiar, their visual spans increase and they read faster. Explain that fluent readers' eyes are ahead of their voices, and they can read faster because their brains already know what is coming in the rest of the sentence.

Prepare a **transparency** of several **sentences** that gradually increase in word count. Place the transparency on the **overhead projector** and cover the sentences. Tell students to look at the first sentence and count the words. Then reveal only the first sentence for just one second each. Ask students to write down how many words they counted. Display each remaining sentence one at a time for just one second each. Invite students to write the number of words they count in each sentence. Repeat the activity over several days with different sentences. Since the activity is designed simply to help students expand their eye span and to discourage word-by-word reading, there is no need to correct responses, but do ask whether students notice the number of words they count increasing over time.

Watch Your Tone

* GIVE MORE PRACTICE IN READING WITH EXPRESSION.

Writing the emphasized words in different colors will get students' attention.

Write a question, such as *What are you doing?* on four sentence strips. On each sentence strip, emphasize a different word by writing it in a different color and using heavy strokes. For example, write **WHAT** *are you doing? What **ARE** you doing? What are **YOU** doing?* and *What are you **DOING**?* Place the sentence strips face down in a pocket chart. Discuss how emphasizing different words can change the meaning of a sentence. Reveal the first sentence strip, and invite students to read the question, emphasizing the highlighted word. Discuss how their tone of voice affected the question. Continue revealing the sentence strips one at a time, and discuss how emphasizing different words affects the overall message of the sentences.

I Mean Business

* FOCUS ON READING IMPERATIVE SENTENCES TO HELP STUDENTS READ WITH EXPRESSION.

Expression gives the text more meaning which makes it easier to remember.

Imperative sentences demand that an action be performed. They are the perfect type of sentence to use for practicing reading with expression. Write several **imperative sentences** on separate **sentence strips**. Create your own or use the following examples: *Give that to me now. Turn off the light. Take the groceries upstairs. Watch out for cars!* (Or use humorous ones, such as *Jump out of the plane, now! Stop eating the dog food! Don't give the monkey a hair cut!* Place a prepared sentence strip in a **pocket chart** and read it in a faint, monotone voice. Read it again using proper intonation and expression. Ask students which version had more meaning. Explain that when reading, students should read like they talk, using emphasis to show what they mean. Continue reading all of the imperative sentences without expression and inviting students to reread them correctly.

Extension: Play a form of Simon Says. Throughout the school day as you tell students to do things, use either the faint, monotone voice or a more expressive, commanding voice. Explain that students should not perform the command unless you use an expressive voice. When you use a monotone voice, let a student reissue the command with appropriate tone and expression.

Helpful Hints

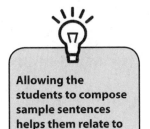

Allowing the students to compose sample sentences helps them relate to the activity.

Directions

Select **sentences** from a text selection, or compose your own that contain clues to the way they should be read, such as *The shy little girl said, "I don't want to go to the House of Monkeys." He smacked his lips and asked his grandmother, "Can I have more chocolate-strawberry milk?" He yelled, "Run! Run away from the giant bugs!"*

Write the preselected sentences on a **transparency**. Explain that students must be on the lookout for clues that will help them understand how to read text. Certain words offer clues about pacing, expression, and tone. Display only the first sentence on the transparency, and ask students to identify clues that indicate how to read the sentence. For example, how would a shy little girl who doesn't want to go somewhere sound? Circle the clue words. Invite students to read the sentence using the appropriate expression or emotion, and then read and discuss the remaining sentences.

Extension: Let students compose their own sample sentences for the class to use during a subsequent practice session.

Word Race

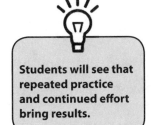

Students will see that repeated practice and continued effort bring results.

Directions

Remind students that by reading the same text repeatedly, they will build their reading speed. Reading becomes more automatic when students immediately recognize words and don't have to decode them. Distribute a copy of the **Long /A/ Word Race reproducible (page 114)** to each student. Tell students to practice reading the words as quickly as possible, moving from one column to the next. Show students how to count the words they read using the totals at the bottom of each column. When students are ready, set a **timer** for one minute and tell students to read as many words as they can until the timer rings. When the timer rings, have students underline the last word they read, count how many words they read, and write their word count totals at the bottom of their pages next to the label *First Reading*. Let students do second and third readings over the next few days with no more that 24 hours between readings. After the third reading, discuss the results and ask why students think the number of words they read increased.

Extension: Create additional word race lists using words that focus on a single phonetic element students are studying. Place the words in five columns of 20 words each.

Partner Reading Checklist

Reader _____

Book Title_____

	1st Reading	2nd Reading	3rd Reading
Listener	_____	_____	_____
# of Hesitations	_____	_____	_____
Expression	_____	_____	_____
Fluency	_____	_____	_____

Scores: **+** = Great!   **/** = OK   **−** = Needs practice

1

- -

Reading Workout Record

Name_____Date _____

Story _____

First Taping: Put a **−** next to the sentences that describe your reading.

I had trouble with some words.   _____
I couldn't figure out some words.   _____
My reading was too slow.   _____
I paused between words and sounded choppy.   _____
I read too fast and couldn't understand the words.   _____
I sounded boring and my voice was flat.   _____

Second Taping: Make a **+** out of every **−** in the areas where you improved.

My reading was better because _____
_____
_____

2

Strategies For Struggling Readers © 2007 Creative Teaching Press

Go-Togethers

Two-Word Phrases

I am	I could	I had	with her
it was	on the	in my	they went
I can	I will	he said	she said
in the	by the	at the	over there

Three-Word Phrases

I will go	you and me	but they are
we went to	I knew that	in your dreams
this is my	by my side	in front of
all day long	in the car	list of words
he did not	when it's time	it was fun
I have a	now I know	in between the
you will see	not this time	add the numbers
here it is	I can't go	circle the word
we like to	with my friend	write your name
yes I will	look at this	list the words
not that way	that was in	identify the one
I like to	it is about	more or less
it is that	come over here	
I think that	in order to	
she said that	to find out	

Long /A/ Word Race

ache	case	haste	pay	shake
age	cave	lace	place	shape
ale	chain	lake	plate	shave
ape	crate	lame	play	snake
ate	date	lane	pray	stage
bail	drain	late	quail	stain
bait	drape	made	quake	stale
bake	face	maid	race	state
base	fake	main	rage	tail
blade	fame	make	rail	take
blame	flake	mane	rain	tame
brace	flame	maze	raise	tape
brain	frail	nail	rake	taste
brake	gain	name	rate	trace
brave	game	page	safe	train
cage	gate	paid	sake	vain
cake	grace	pail	same	wade
came	grade	pain	save	wait
cane	grain	paste	scrape	wake
cape	grape	pave	shade	wave
20	40	60	80	100

First Reading   _____ words   _____ date

Second Reading   _____ words   _____ date

Third Reading   _____ words   _____ date

Comprehension

Comprehension—constructing meaning from print—is the ultimate goal of reading. The most basic type of comprehension is explicit comprehension, where meaning is direct, clear, and unambiguous. A more sophisticated form, implicit comprehension, requires the reader to think beyond what the text explicitly says to make inferences and understand underlying intent. Students must develop strategies to gain both types of meaning.

Just as each student needs to develop word-learning strategies, he or she must also rely on comprehension strategies in order to retain, interact with, and process text. These strategies need to become part of each student's unconscious reading process so that he or she can combine and apply strategies to problem solve and interpret text before, during, and after reading. Many struggling readers have graphophonic, semantic, or syntactic difficulties that impede their reading and comprehension process. The following skill-based comprehension activities use specific instructional techniques, rather than general reading strategies, to help struggling readers focus on major comprehension pitfalls.

Prerequisite Skills in Comprehension

In order to gain meaning from text and remember what was read, at-risk readers need to do the following:

- Develop automatic word recognition skills.
- Examine text features, skim to get a sense of what the text is about, and identify/preview organizational structure.
- Connect what they already know about the topic and form related opinions based upon experiences and prior knowledge.
- Make predictions using clues from the title, illustrations, and text details.
- Interact with the text by asking questions to review content and to connect old and new learning about the topic.
- Identify, organize, and draw conclusions about essential information in the text.

Recommendations

As a teacher, your role in the reading process is to create experiences and environments that introduce, nurture, or extend students' abilities to engage with text. This means that you must engage in explicit instruction, modeling, scaffolding, facilitation, and participation. To do this, you must have a firm grasp of the content presented in the text and relate it to struggling readers' individual needs. Note that instruction of comprehension strategies may not be effective until mechanical problems typical of struggling readers are corrected. If a student does not understand things like passive voice, relationships between clauses, or how to monitor their reading, then using a comprehension strategy may be pointless. Evaluate each students' needs and adjust instruction accordingly.

Click and Clank

*TEACH STUDENTS TO SELF-MONITOR THEIR READING IN ORDER TO IMPROVE TEXT UNDERSTANDING.

As students practice this activity, they will learn to monitor their reading to see if it makes sense.

Directions ▶ Choose a **text selection** and substitute key words with incorrect or nonsense words that are visually similar or have a subtle phonetic change. For example, change *wanted* to *wented* and *laws* to *lawns*. Practice reading the passage with the miscues so that it sounds natural. (See example below.)

*He was **ejected** as senator and went to Washington D.C. As a senator he worked on the **lawns** of our country. But it was not always that **why**. Before John Glenn was **walking** with problems of this **word**, he was in outer **spake**. In February 1962, he became the **fist** American to **trivia** in the earth's orbit. He had **anyways** wanted to be an astronaut.*

Explain that when reading, students can be clicking right along when suddenly there is a *clank*— something that doesn't sound right. That *clank* means that the passage doesn't make sense. Explain that by training themselves to listen when they read (monitoring their own reading), they can hear mistakes and correct them. Next, read aloud a passage and pause slightly after each mistake to give students a chance to respond. When something doesn't sound right, students should say *clank*. After students say *clank,* ask what the word should be. Eventually, students should say *clank* and then the correct word without being prompted. This helps maintain the storyline by keeping the interruption minimal.

Once students easily find miscues as you read aloud, assign them to independently read a short passage containing miscues. (Students will now combine auditory and visual learning to find the mistakes.) If students falter a bit at the beginning, provide support by revealing the number of miscues in the passage. Repeat with additional passages from students' reading to reinforce word recognition and comprehension. Note that as students practice this activity, their ability to find the miscues will first increase but then decrease. The decrease means that students are automatically correcting the mistakes and have learned to monitor their reading.

My Mind Went Blank

*TEACH STUDENTS TO SELF-MONITOR THEIR READING TO IMPROVE THEIR UNDERSTANDING.

Using close sentences helps the student see how they can use what they know to remember other ideas and events.

Directions ▶ Write a short **summary of a story** that includes all of the main ideas. Choose several words that will require students to reflect on what happened in the story, and substitute them with blanks. Copy a class set of the cloze passage. Tell students that you started to write a summary of a story but your mind went blank. Invite students to read the summary and fill in the blanks using markers. Encourage them to refer to the original story to make sure that their spelling is correct.

Most Important Ideas (MIIs)

 **Directions** ▶ Choose a **text selection** with an illustration on the first page. Have students study the illustration and determine the most important part of the picture. Tell the students, as they read the story, to think about the most important parts. While students are reading the text, write the most important ideas (not the full sentences) from the first few pages on different **sentence strips**. Provide additional **sentence strips** and **markers**. After students have read the text, introduce MIIs—**m**ost **i**mportant **i**deas. When students have selected the MII, display the first teacher-made MII sentence strip on a bulletin board or in a pocket chart. Have students continue finding MIIs on each of the first few pages until all sentence strips are displayed. After modeling this format, assign each student to finish reading one page of the remaining text and show you the MII.

If a student is correct, give him or her a sentence strip and a marker and have the student write the MII and the page number. As students finish, add their sentence strips to the display until all pages from the text are represented. Have students take turns reading the sentence strips in order and then use those words to retell what happened on that page.

Starting this assignment with an illustration as well as text will help keep students' attention. Allowing students to choose the words from their reading lets them assign importance to the information.

Extension: Use the sentence strips in a writing lesson on sentence fragments. Have students select a few of the sentence strips and write complete sentences using the words written on them. Allow students to share their completed sentences in sequence.

Concept Box

Using pictures helps reinforce both old and new learning.

Directions ▶ Plan some questions that relate to a **text selection** students will read. The questions should be simple enough for students to use prior knowledge to answer without having read the text. Ask the questions, let students answer them, and then ask how students know the answers if they have not yet read the text. Explain that what students already know is called *prior knowledge*, and prior knowledge helps readers understand ideas in a story. When reading, readers combine old learning (what they already know) with new learning (what they are learning in the story). Place the transparency of the **Concept Box reproducible (page 124)** on the overhead projector and distribute a copy to each student. Tell students that before reading about a topic, they should think about what they already know, and the Concept Box reproducible will help them to do that.

For example, if the reading selection topic is about life cycles, ask students to think about what they already know about the life cycle of a butterfly. As students answer, write the topic on the line at the top of the transparency, have students do the same, and begin drawing pictures in the boxes to illustrate what is being discussed. Have students simultaneously draw and label pictures to show their prior knowledge. When students have finished drawing, draw a thick, vertical line between the last illustrated picture box and the first empty one. Have students do the same. Tell students that as they read and encounter new information, they should illustrate that new information in the remaining, empty sections of their concept boxes. Read the story aloud together, and then let students read

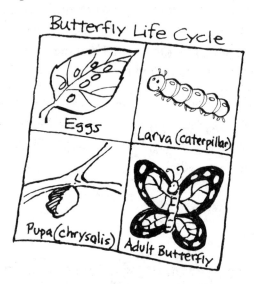

the story independently and complete their concept boxes. Ask volunteers to share the pictures in their concept boxes and identify what prior knowledge and new information those pictures represent.

Shrink It

* ENCOURAGE STUDENTS TO DEVELOP CONCISE AND EFFECTIVE STORY SUMMARIES.

Using a spinner adds novelty to this challenging task.

 **Directions** ▶ Assign a brief text selection for students to read prior to this activity. Make several copies of the **Shrink It Spinner and arrow (page 125)** on cardstock. Cut out the game boards and arrows. Attach each arrow to the center of a game board using a brass fastener. Make sure that the spinner spins easily; if it gets stuck, enlarge the hole for the brass fastener. Next, invite students to orally summarize the story. Tell students that their ideas were all correct, but assuming the summary was very lengthy, ask what could be left out to make it shorter. As students respond, point out that they are deleting details—parts of the story that made it interesting but were not significant. Tell students that they will have to shrink the summary small enough to fit into a nutshell—only main ideas can go into the summary. After students share the main ideas, ask them if all that would fit in a nutshell. Tell them that they will have to shrink the summary even more. Guide students to determine the overall meaning or theme of the story. Have them concentrate on what significant event (the main problem) happened in the beginning, what resulted from this, and how the story ended.

Helping students develop an oral summary statement may require extensive practice using different text selections. Once students are able to determine the overall theme of a story, have them write summary statements in small groups. Have students spin the **Shrink It Spinner** to determine how many words they can use in their summary statements. Each group should then summarize the story and shrink it so that it contains the correct number of words.

Picture It

* BUILD STUDENTS' WORKING MEMORIES AND HELP THEM APPLY THAT SKILL TO REMEMBERING TEXT.

Students see that visualizing, making mental pictures, helps them remember what they read.

 **Directions** ▶ Choose a text selection that can be easily illustrated. Remind students that the working memory can only hold a limited amount of information. Discuss how to increase the working memory's capacity by chunking information together. Repeat a chunking activity from the *My Brain Booklet* **(pages 11–12, script pages 25–26)**. Next, explain that the same thing happens when students try to remember what they read. Sometimes there is too much information for the working memory to hold. Tell students that when they read, they have to chunk ideas together and come up with the overall idea.

Read a **text selection** aloud, and then invite each student to draw a picture that represents the overall meaning of the text. Have a few volunteers share their illustrations and discuss how all of the important information from the passage was chunked together into one picture. The pictures will help their working memories recall the meaning of the text. However, if a picture were drawn for every sentence in the passage, the working memory would be too overloaded to remember all of the pictures.

First and Last

* HELP STUDENTS CONTINUE TO LEARN HOW TO BUILD THEIR WORKING MEMORIES.

Students use visual images to remember the "gist," or important points, in text.

 **Directions** ➤ Explain that some readers have difficulty remembering a number of words at one time. They may be reading a sentence, and by the time they get to the end of the sentence, they have forgotten what the first part of the sentence said. Once again, students need to help their working memory remember things. Tell students that they are going to help strengthen their working memories by using pictures. Read a two-part sentence that offers two ideas. After hearing the first idea, students should quickly make a simple sketch to help them remember it. At the same time, they must listen to the last part of the sentence to hear the second idea and sketch something to help them remember it. Read the first sentence from a **text selection**, or use the following sentence.

The scrawny little dog ran into the yard, circled the tree, and headed for the porch looking for food.

Discuss student drawings, which may be simple illustrations of a dog and food. Remind them to draw quick and simple pictures so that they can move on to draw the next picture. Continue the activity by adding sentences to create an entire paragraph, having students continue to draw and listen as they work to improve their sentence comprehension.

The scrawny little dog ran into the yard, circled the tree, and headed for the porch looking for food. When he found nothing but the newspaper on the porch, he picked up the newspaper and angrily began tearing it apart. I knew right away that I would be the one who had to clean it up. At that moment, I wished that the dog I found was a neat and tidy little kitty cat.

Find and Identify

* TRAIN STUDENTS TO UNDERSTAND THE IMPORTANCE OF WORD ORDER WHEN DETERMINING SENTENCE MEANING.

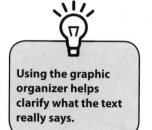

Using the graphic organizer helps clarify what the text really says.

 **Directions** ➤ Choose some sentences from a current **text selection** and give each student a copy of the **Who Did What? reproducible (page 126)**. Read each sentence aloud. Have students independently identify the subject, the verb, and the object in each and then write the sentence parts in the appropriate sections of their reproducibles. Discuss students' responses and clarify any confusion.

Extension: This activity can also be done as a partner or small group activity. Assign a paragraph to each pair or small group. Have students identify the subject, the verb, and the object, and record them in the appropriate sections of their reproducibles.

Who Did What?

Using color to label the sentence parts will draw attention to them and help students remember the categories for each part.

 **Directions**

Compose or select some **sentences** from students' reading material that follow the subject, verb, object (SVO) order, such as *The cat ate the tuna.* Make a **transparency** of these sentences, and provide a copy for each student. Tell students to be sentence detectives and figure out who did what. To do so, they will need to find the subject (S), the verb (V), and the object (O) of each sentence and label them accordingly. Use the transparency to demonstrate how to find the S, V, O. Use a different color to label each part of the sentence. After marking a few of the sentences together, distribute the student copies. Invite students to mark the subject, verb, and object of each sentence.

Extension: When students are ready for a challenge, have them practice labeling the S, V, and O in sentences with prepositional phrases, such as, *The cat ate the tuna after drinking milk,* and *The cat ate the tuna under the table.*

Flip It

Color-coding the sentence parts with different colors will help students recognize how the meanings stay the same, even when the order of the parts of the sentences is different.

 **Directions**

Provide students with colored pencils or markers. In advance, write some **sentences** that follow the subject-verb-object order in black ink on a **transparency.** Leave enough space between the sentences to label and then rewrite each sentence. Possible examples include the following:

The truck towed a boat.   *A famous artist painted that picture.*
The farmer plowed the field.   *My cousin won the contest.*
My favorite movie is Shrek.   *My mother answered the phone.*

Passive voice can be confusing and difficult for students to understand. Provide multiple opportunities for students to improve their understanding of this concept. Discuss the subject-verb-object order in the sentences. Have students read the sentences and identify each subject, verb, and object. Mark the subjects with red, the verbs with blue, and the objects with green. Explain that when the subject of the sentence comes first, the sentence is written in *active voice.*

Next, ask students if this order must be followed in every sentence. Rewrite some of the sentences, putting the objects first. For example, write *The boat was towed by the truck.* and *That picture was painted by a famous artist.* As you label the subjects, verbs, and objects with markers, explain that if the object of the sentence comes first, the sentence is written in *passive voice.* Invite students to flip the remaining sentences by rewriting them and putting the objects first. Have them label the parts with the same colors used earlier as they work.

Who Are You Talking About?

*TEACH STUDENTS TO IDENTIFY CLAUSES TO HELP THEM UNDERSTAND LONG SENTENCES.

This activity helps students understand confusing clauses by identifying subjects and their referral words. As a result, students better understand the meaning of the sentence.

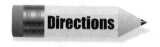 **Directions**

Many struggling readers, especially second language learners, tend to match referral words to the closest nouns. It is important to give extended practice with *referral* words. Make a list of **sentences** with multiple clauses, such as *The boy rode the bike that belonged to the neighbor all by himself. The mother dog that took her puppies outside wanted them to stay close to her. While my mother was out shopping, my sister jumped on my mother's bed and sprained her ankle. Even though they were nervous about their routine, the cheerleaders performed well for the judges.* Make a **transparency** of these sentences and a copy for each student.

As you display the transparency, read the first sentence. Ask *Who is this sentence talking about?* After students identify the subject (*boy*), ask how many times the boy is referred to in the sentence. Draw an arrow from the word *himself* back to the word *boy*. Explain that in long sentences, it is easy to get mixed up because there are so many words. Sometimes the subject is at the beginning of the sentence and the *referral* word is at the end. While the word *himself* is close to the word *neighbor*, it refers to the subject at the beginning of the sentence (*boy*). Continue with more of the sentences. When students are able to match each subject and *referral* word, distribute the copies of the sentences. Have students read them and draw an arrow from each *referral* word to its subject.

Extension: Choose additional sentences with multiple clauses from students' reading. Once students begin to recognize these sentences, allow them to submit additional ones from their reading for you to use in giving them more practice with this skill.

Sentence Stretchers

* CONTINUE WORKING WITH STUDENTS TO IDENTIFY CLAUSES.

Making up sentences about student brings novelty to the activity. Writing and reading silently and reading aloud provide multiple modes of learning.

 **Directions** ➤ Begin by talking to students about how easy it is to "get lost" in long sentences. Give an example, such as *Juan, a student in my class, likes to play soccer on Saturdays with his team, the Giants, who have won every game this season.*

Ask students to identify the most important idea in this sentence. Point out that because there is so much information, it may be hard to identify the main idea that Juan likes to play soccer. Create some simple sentences about students and write them on the board. Leave enough space under each sentence to write an additional sentence. Have students read aloud the first sentence you have written on the board. Invite students to stretch the sentence by adding more details. Write the new sentence underneath the first one. For example, write *Mariella loves to dance*. Then write *Mariella, who sits in the front row, loves to dance and takes ballet classes after school*. Have students read both sentences. Explain that both have the same main idea, but the second sentences provide more information. Explain that the reader sometimes has to "dig through" the words in a sentence to find the main point. By reading the main idea sentence first and then adding additional information, students can see how extra words don't change the core meaning. Invite students to read and stretch each sentence on the board.

Extension: Let students complete this exercise independently by writing and stretching a sentence about each of their classmates. Collect the sentences and choose one from each student about another student, so that each student is represented both by a sentence he or she wrote and one that is written about him or her. Mark your sentence choice on each student's paper, and have all students share their sentences with the class.

Name: _____

Concept Box

Directions: Draw pictures to show what you already know about the topic. Label your drawings. Draw a thick line after the last picture you draw. As you read the story, draw pictures of new information you discover in the remaining boxes. Label these new drawings.

TOPIC _____

Old Learning

New Learning

Strategies For Struggling Readers © 2007 Creative Teaching Press

Name:_____

Shrink It Spinner

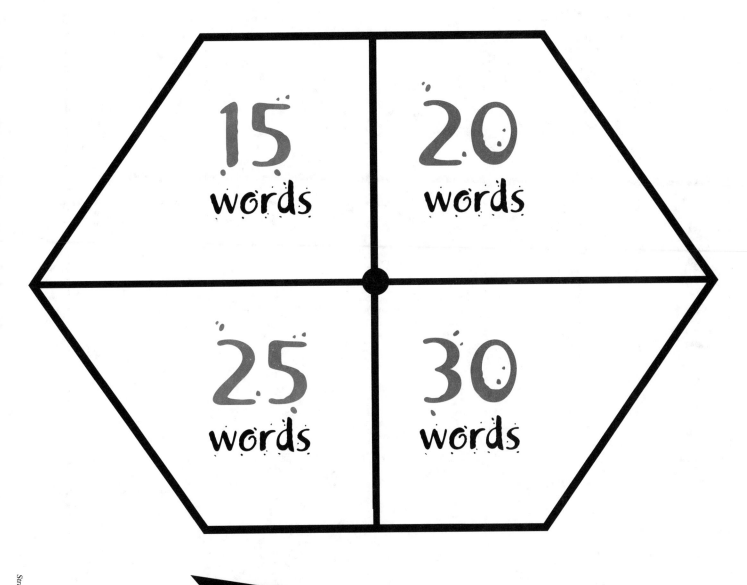

Name: _____

Who Did What?

Directions: Find and identify the subject, the verb, and the object in each sentence. Write them in the appropriate sections.

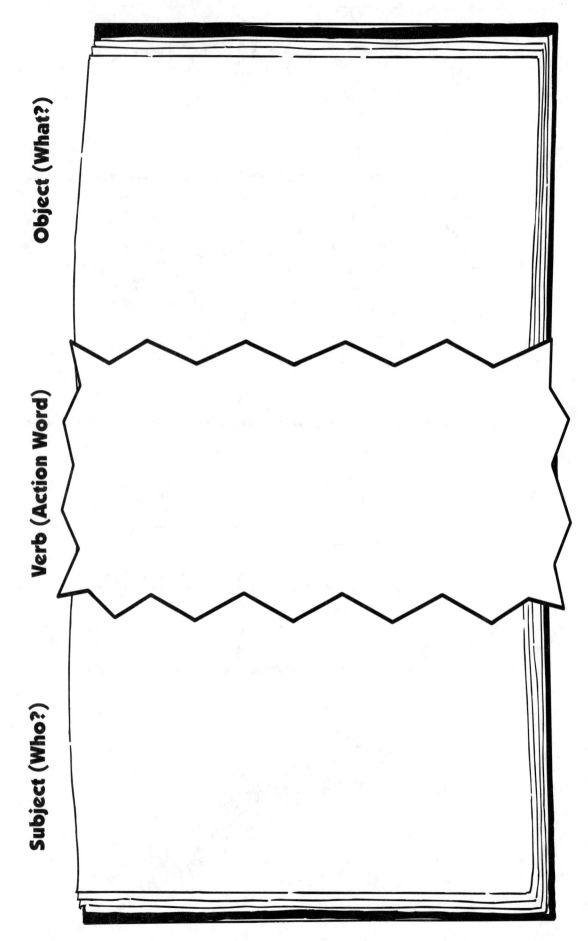

Subject (Who?)

Verb (Action Word)

Object (What?)

Citations

Allington, Richard, "Critical Factors in Designing an Effective Reading Intervention for Struggling Readers," in *Understanding and Implementing Reading First Initiatives: The Changing Role of Administrators*, ed. Carrice Cummins (Newark, DE: International Reading Association, 2006).

Armbruster, Bonnie B., Fran Lehr, and Jean Osborn, *Put Reading First: The Research Building Blocks for Teaching Children to Read* (Washington, D. C.: National Institute for Literacy, 2001).

Bender, William N., *Differentiating Instruction for Students with Learning Disabilities* (Thousand Oaks, CA: Corwin Press, 2002).

Braunger, Jane, and Jan Patricia Lewis, *Building a Knowledge Base in Reading* (Newark, DE: International Reading Association, 2006).

Committee on the Prevention of Reading Difficulties in Young Children, *Preventing Reading Difficulties in Young Children*, eds. Catherine E. Snow, M. Susan Burns, Peg Griffin (Washington, D.C.: National Academy Press, 1998).

Cummins, Carrice, ed., *Understanding and Implementing Reading First Initiatives: The Changing Role of Administrators* (Newark, DE: International Reading Association, 2006).

Farstrup, Alan E., and Samuels, S. Jay, eds., *What Research Has to Say About Reading Instruction* (Newark, DE: International Reading Association, 2002).

Guthrie, John T., "Teaching for Literacy Engagement," *Journal of Literacy Research 36, no. 1* (Spring 2004): 1-29.

Guthrie, John T., William D. Schafer, and Chun-Wei Huang., "Benefits of Opportunity to Read and Balanced Instruction," *The Journal of Educational Research* 94, no. 3 (2001):145-162.

Jensen, Eric, *Brain-Based Learning: The New Science of Teaching and Training* (San Diego: Brain Store, Inc., 1995).

Kaufeldt, Martha, *Begin with the Brain: Orchestrating the Learner-Centered Classroom* (Tucson: Zephyr Press, 1999).

Lehr, Fran, and Jean Osborn, *A Focus on Comprehension: Research-Based Practices in Early Reading Series* (Honolulu: Pacific Resources for Education and Learning, 2005).

Citations

Samuels, S. Jay, and Alan E. Farstrup, eds., *What Research Has to Say About Fluency Instruction* (Newark, DE: International Reading Association, 2006).

Sousa, David, *How the Brain Learns to Read* (Thousand Oaks, CA: Corwin Press, 2005).

Sousa, David, *How the Brain Learns* (Thousand Oaks, CA: Corwin Press, 2006).

Tileston, Donna Walker, *What Every Teacher Should Know About Learning, Memory, and the Brain* (Thousand Oaks, CA: Corwin Press, 2001).

Wolfe, Patricia, *Brain Matters: Translating Research into Classroom Practice* (Alexandria, VA: Association for Supervision and Curriculum Development, 2001).